The Important Role
of the
IRISH
in the
American
Revolution

Dr. Phillip Thomas Tucker

HERITAGE BOOKS
2009

HERITAGE BOOKS
AN IMPRINT OF HERITAGE BOOKS, INC.

Books, CDs, and more—Worldwide

For our listing of thousands of titles see our website
at
www.HeritageBooks.com

Published 2009 by
HERITAGE BOOKS, INC.
Publishing Division
100 Railroad Ave. #104
Westminster, Maryland 21157

International Standard Book Numbers
Paperbound: 978-0-7884-5018-1
Clothbound: 978-0-7884-8236-6

For the Cox Family of Missouri
And
Their Distinguished Scotch-Irish Ancestors

Table of Contents

Acknowledgments

Many sincere thanks go to a good many people who provided not only direct assistance but also inspiration. First, I would like to thank Mr. Thomas J. Fleming, America's preeminent Revolutionary War historian and authority, for his inspirational works about the American Revolution over many years, and especially his classic study, *Washington's Secret War*. In this fine work, he revealed the importance of the widespread Irish contribution from recently discovered primary sources.

And I would like to thank Mr. George Gibson who also helped to inspire my research into the long-overlooked story of the Irish in the American Revolution. Both Mr. Fleming and Gibson fully understand and appreciate the important role played by the Irish from 1775 to 1783.

Introduction

No single chapter of American history has been steeped in more mythology than the American Revolution. Almost from the beginning, the birth of the American republic in violent revolution has been transformed into romantic legend of mythical proportions, along with its heroes, especially George Washington. In a process of romanticization that has continued unabated to this day, the Founding Fathers have become immortalized by generations of Americans, looming larger than life and more mythical than real.

But one group of colonial Americans have remained noticeably absent from the dramatic story of the American Revolution, the Irish and the Scotch-Irish. By any measure, the Irish and Scotch-Irish soldier have become the forgotten man of the American Revolution in large part because of their generally lowly social and economic status in colonial society. Besides African Americans in bondage, no people in colonial America held a lower rung of the social order than the Irish and Scotch-Irish, especially recent immigrants.

The fact that the Irish and Scotch-Irish have become the forgotten patriots of the American Revolution has been especially ironic, because they made seemingly endless vital contributions to the cause of independence that were not only disproportionate and important, but also decisive. In the analysis of one high-ranking French officer, Marquis de Chastellux, who fought beside General Washington's forces during the Yorktown campaign: the Continental "Congress owed its existence, and America probably her preservation, to the fidelity and firmness of the Irish." This opinion of this French major general was right on target and not an exaggeration.

However, the story of the Irish in the American Revolution has been most elusive. Indeed, the vast majority of the Irish immigrants in colonial America were mostly

9

illiterate, leaving few records of his contributions, both on and off the battlefield. Consequently, the Celtic-Gaelic fighting man in America became the most overlooked participant of the American Revolution. Only recently has this lack of recognition for the Irish contributions begun to change. In 2005 and after extensive research into primary sources, historian Thomas J. Fleming revealed the undeniable truth in his classic work *Washington's Secret War, The Hidden History of Valley Forge*. In this ground-breaking book, Fleming ascertained that at Valley Forge during the winter of 1777-1778, Washington's Continental Army consisted of a large percentage of Irish. In Fleming's words: "Perhaps the most surprising thing about the soldiers was the number of foreign born-men in the ranks [and] By far the highest percentage of these newcomers were Irish."

Fleming also emphasized how a full "two-fifths of the Continental Army" was Irish by May 1778. Interestingly, Fleming's recent discoveries about the sizeable Irish composition of the Continental Army was in fact nothing new. Ironically, a good many high-ranking American and British leaders, both military and political, were fully aware of the large percentage of Irish in Washington's ranks and the important contributions of these Celtic-Gaelic soldiers throughout the war years.

The famed Pennsylvania Line, one of the hardest-fighting commands of Washington's Army, contained such a sizeable percentage of Irish troops that this elite unit became widely known as the "Line of Ireland." And General Charles Lee, Washington's second in command before the 1776 Trenton Campaign, was fully convinced and firmly "believed half the rebel army [Washington's Continental Army] were from Ireland."

But the important Irish and Scotch-Irish contributions in the struggle for independence were not solely confined to Washington's Army. Large percentages of Irish and Scotch-

Irish troops won distinction in the Southern theater, including such battles as Cowpens and Kings Mountain. Consequently, the fascinating story of the Irish and Scotch-Irish role in playing such an overall large and key role in winning a new nation's independence has been described in detail by the representative battles presented in this work.

Because no definitive works have been devoted to the full story of the disproportionate Irish and Scotch Irish accomplishments in the American Revolution, key representative examples of their contributions in the most important battles have been illuminated in this work.

Chapter I: America's First Foreign Invasion, the Assault on Quebec December 1775

Perhaps no better example of the significance of the Irish role in the American Revolution can be seen than in the case of America's first invasion of foreign soil, Canada. In overall symbolic terms, therefore, it was appropriate that the capable American leader of the Canadian invasion was a promising Ireland-born commander, General Richard Montgomery. General Montgomery would become the first patriot general killed in the American Revolution, falling to rise no more on Canadian soil, after capturing Montreal, Canada. The tall, handsome General Montgomery possessed much solid military experience when the lack of experience was a hallmark among an unprofessional American leadership corps at the war's beginning.

By only the slimmest of margins in keeping a small, ill-equipped, and ragtag colonial army together on the lengthy, arduous march north by his own leadership ability in the harshest conditions, General Montgomery just narrowly missed capturing the capital of Canada, Quebec, and transforming Canada into the fourteenth American colony. This gifted Ireland-born general gave his life for almost achieving that lofty national goal as ordained by the new Continental Congress. Had not General Montgomery been killed in the snows of Quebec city, not only Quebec but also Canada would almost certainly become part of the United States. Indeed, the bold, erudite Irishman fell at the head of his troops, dying a lonely death in a bloody snowdrift far from home, when on the very threshold of America's most dramatic strategic success to date.

Montgomery was a transplanted revolutionary by the time of the American Revolution. Like so many other Irish immigrants, America was his adopted homeland. On December 2, 1738, Montgomery was born on the family country estate in County Dublin in east central Ireland. His prosperous father was a privileged member of the Irish gentry, and a respected Irish Parliamentary member. The elder Montgomery also possessed a fine military record, serving as a source of inspiration for the young man of promise. The Montgomery family proudly traced its distinguished ancestry back to the Normans of France. But the family migrated to England and converted from Catholicism to Calvinist Protestantism. One of the most famous Montgomery family members was a hard-fighting Huguenot general, who battled French Catholics to win distinction.

A more direct Richard Montgomery descendant, Sir Hugh Montgomery, served against the rebellious native Irish Catholics, who were defending their Green Isle homeland and ancestral way-of-life against the interloping English during 1689-1691. Like other English commanders who helped to vanquish the Irish, Montgomery gained extensive amounts of confiscated Irish lands as a reward for his distinguished military service. Such spoils of war from Ireland's conquest became the central foundation of the Montgomery family's subsequent prestige and wealth, sustaining future generations.

Young Richard Montgomery, therefore, benefitted directly from his ancestors' successes in crushing the native Irish revolts across the Emerald isle. He gained a fine education at Ireland's leading educational institution, Trinity College in Dublin. Like his ambitious ancestors before him, Richard aspired to make a distinguished name for himself with a military career. Therefore, as was customary for the upper classes of England in the Eighteenth Century, his father purchased an ensign's commission for his son in a British regiment. Montgomery then entered the British Army as an officer in 1756 at age eighteen. He then embarked upon a most promising career with a historic Irish regiment, the Seventeenth Regiment of Foot, which served in America during the French and Indian Wars.

Montgomery gained his first combat experience with his regiment during the siege of Louisbourg in 1757. The most powerful French fortress on the continent, Louisbourg was of great strategic value in the struggle for mastery of the North America. Louisbourg's capture would allow any British invasion force easy entry into the St. Lawrence River to invade the heart of New France, including the city of Quebec. Louisbourg surrendered to the British and American colonial allies in the summer of 1757. Ironically, the next time that Montgomery was destined to serve on Canadian soil would be as a high-ranking rebel officer against the King, who he once had served so faithfully in Canada.

After Louisbourg's fall, Montgomery continued his tour of duty in America, in New York, with his regiment of redcoats, and in British campaigns during the geopolitical struggle for possession of the rich French sugar islands in the West Indies. However, the omnipresent intrigue of regimental politics suddenly intervened to end Montgomery's chances for a more promising military career in April 1772. A frustrated Montgomery, therefore, quit the British Army in disgust, after the old familiar formula of more money and higher political connections for less competent sons of the wealthy so often proved more important in determining a successful military career in the British military than individual merit and accomplishment.

Seeking a fresh start far away from the world of British Army politics and a dead-end military career, Montgomery migrated from England to New York to begin life anew. Here, he become a gentleman-farmer just north of New York City among the fertile lands along the wide Hudson River at King's Bridge, New York. More important for his social aspirations, Montgomery married into one of the elite political families of New York, the powerful

14

Livingston family, wedding Janet Livingston in 1773. The Emerald Islander gained not only a beautiful wife, but also a fortune with his influential marriage.

When New York's patriots formed the Provincial Congress in New York, Montgomery served as a delegate. Despite his former service in the British Army, he was a natural revolutionary, revealing an unconventional nature. With colonial preparations for open conflict with the Mother Country reaching fever-pitch, Montgomery's belief in America's self-determination and bright future combined with his extensive military experience to ensure that he would play a leading role in the upcoming conflict. Despite in part haunted by the fact that he might have to face his former comrades and friends of his old British regiment on a future battlefield, Montgomery accepted a general's commission and prepared for war.

Overconfident about the formidable task ahead, naive Congress members decided to launch an invasion of Canada. Envisioning glory for American arms in Canada, these politicians fully expected an easy victory and the swift addition of a fourteenth colony. Indeed, hardly had the Continental Army been created on June 17, 1775, when Congress had turned its eyes to the great prize of Canada. Positioned near the Canadian border in New York, General Montgomery and his New York troops were destined to play a leading role in the winter 1775 campaign in Canada. Based upon the ill-founded concept of "liberating" a French Canadian people under British rule through the appeal of republican and revolutionary principles combined with Montgomery's sword, Congress' ambitious plan to launch America's first foreign invasion effort was as over-optimistic as it was grandiose.

For the undertaking of mounting an invasion of Canada, Congress raised 3,000 Continental troops for the audacious winter campaign. A good many of these patriot soldiers who

General Montgomery commanded during the invasion of Canada, including the Green Mountain Boys from Vermont, were Irish and Scotch-Irish. Unlike the aristocratic officers of higher social standing, the common soldiers in the ranks were for the most part poor, including many recent immigrants from Ireland, indentured servants, and yeoman farmers. While the Irish from New York City were mostly common laborers, the Irish from the surrounding frontier regions of New York State were primarily farm laborers and small farmers. At this time, the largest concentration of Scotch-Irish were located in the appropriately named counties of Orange and Ulster, New York, situated west of the mighty Hudson River. Located on the western and northern frontiers, many of these Celtic-Gaelic warriors possessed ample French and Indian War experience.

In this yet frontier region, the initial unit raised for military service was the First New York Regiment, which was organized in 1775's summer. This fine regiment was commanded by Scotland-born Colonel Alexander McDougall, a combative and popular Celtic leader known for a fiery temper. Having migrated to America with his family at age six, Colonel McDougall led a good many Irish and Scotch-Irish soldiers from the New York counties of Albany, Tryon, Charlotte, and Cumberland. And the Third New York Regiment was so thoroughly Scotch-Irish, with its members chiefly from the Province of Ulster, Northern Ireland, that it was nicknamed the Ulster Regiment.

Highly motivated, in his own words, by "the Glorious Cause of America," General Montgomery molded these zealous young soldiers into an effective fighting force. The Irishman prepared them to undertake the daunting challenge of America's first invasion of foreign soil, the conquest of Canada. High-spirited and feisty, the Irish and Scotch-Irish soldiers were eager to launch this ambitious invasion far to the north. Most of all, they were determined to drive British

Regulars from Canada to eliminate what had been a longtime threat to the New York frontier.

Not only Ulster County, but also nearly Orange County, New York, were frontier regions most populated by "the sons and grandsons of the County Longford [Ireland] Irish who had come to America" with such high hopes for a brighter future. Orange County had been named in honor of King William of Orange who won his decisive victory in southeast Ireland, not far from the Irish Sea, over the exiled King of England James II and his Irish Catholic allies at the battle of the Boyne in 1690 to ensure Protestant domination in Ireland and Catholic decline in Ireland.

These hardy young men and boys from far-away Ireland now served in the New York companies and regiments in disproportionately high numbers. However, some of the largest number of Irish soldiers in Montgomery's invasion force were not just from New York. A good many other Irishmen and Scotch-Irish served under the command of Ireland-born Captain Daniel Morgan. He led three companies of sharpshooting "Irish riflemen" from the western frontier of Maryland and Pennsylvania. These Celtic-Gaelic warriors were destined by become the "eyes and ears" of the invasion force during its thrust to Canada

In addition, a good many Irish of Rhode Island also served in the ranks of those planning to conquer Canada. For instance, the company of Captain Simeon Thayer, of Providence, included large numbers of Irish, who now served under Colonel Benedict Arnold. Arnold commanded the other wing of the invasion force dispatched to conquer Canada, while General Montgomery led the principal invasion force which initially targeted Montreal, after taking command from General Philip Schuyler. But Montgomery held overall command of the invasion of Canada.

To attend to the sick and wounded, Dr. Isaac Senter, from the Irish settlement of Londonderry, New Hampshire, which was named in honor of the town of Londonderry in northern Ireland, served as a surgeon of the Continental Line. Both Captain Thayer and Dr. Senter were destined to be captured in the forthcoming debacle at Quebec.

The strategic plan to invade Canada involved a two-pronged offensive effort by two American forces that was calculated to cause the dispersal of the limited number of British forces, which included a high percentage of Irish, to protect both Montreal and Quebec: a virtual impossibility for the defenders because of logistics, space, and geography. While Arnold's force, the right wing, advanced northwest through the untamed wilderness of upper Massachusetts--now Maine--by way of the Kennebec and Chaudiere Rivers and advanced on Quebec and a grueling march of more than 300 miles, General Montgomery's column, the left wing of the invasion force, pushed toward Montreal from the southwest. General Montgomery won the invasion's first dividends with the capture of the stone bastion known as Fort Chambly, located just north of St. Johns and slightly southeast of Montreal, which was situated on the St. Lawrence River southwest of Quebec. Here, at Fort Chambly just north of St. Johns, the first British flag of the war was taken by American troops, when they captured the silk colors of the Seventh Regiment, or the Seventh Royal Fusiliers.

After a lengthy siege from early September to early November that cost much precious time because of winter's approach, the British fort at St. Johns on the Richelieu River surrendered to General Montgomery, who reaped yet another victory. With the capture of Fort Chambly and St. Johns, Montgomery had gained the first two victories won by the infant Continental Army, since its formation less than six months before.

Assisted by his faithful Irish aide-de-camp Captain John MacPherson, Montgomery led the advance on Montreal with renewed confidence for success. On November 13, he captured Montreal and accepted its surrender. At this point, General Montgomery, the former redcoat officer who had once served England so faithfully, had reaped such a relatively easy success that he exclaimed: "I blush for his Majesty's troops!" This Irishman felt no great joy in conquering those men in red uniforms from both England and Ireland.

Exploiting the momentum of his success and knowing that he had to move swiftly to exploit it before winter's onset, Montgomery then set his sights on the greatest prize in all of Canada, the strategic city of Quebec nearly two hundred miles to the northeast. Therefore, General Montgomery continued to lead his army northeast along the wide St. Lawrence and toward Quebec. Ironically, now energetically attempting to galvanize a solid defense to a fellow Irishman's looming threat was the British governor of Quebec, Sir Guy Carleton. A member of the Irish Protestant upper class, he was born in Strabane, County Tryone, Ireland, near where General Montgomery was born on the Emerald Isle. Sir Carleton and General Montgomery had served together as fellow British officers in the French and Indian Wars.

Despite harsh winter weather and the lack of provisions that caused much suffering among the ill-clad American troops during the lengthy march northeast toward Quebec, Montgomery kept his increasingly disgruntled men together by sheer force of will and character. In the bitter cold, Montgomery might have thought about those past 1762 tropical campaigns that resulted in the British capture of Havana, Cuba, and the island of the Martinique in the warm Caribbean, when he had been a younger man. Even when General Montgomery's forces linked with Colonel Arnold's army for a combined total of just more than 1,100 soldiers on December 2, 1775, this united command was yet far too small for the stiff challenge of overwhelming formidable

Quebec, especially so late in the year when in winter's grip.

Even worse, the Emerald Islander lacked heavy siege artillery to reduce the walled, heavily-fortified Quebec with a lengthy siege. Bluff and bluster by Montgomery failed to produce Carleton's surrender. Clearly, the British were prepared to defend Quebec to the bitter end. Ironically, because Montgomery would not contemplate withdrawal from Quebec or Canada, only one recourse remained for any chance that Canada might yet become the Fourteenth Colony.

Consequently, General Montgomery was now forced by fate and circumstance to attempt to do what was virtually impossible and against his inclinations: the launching of an assault in a desperate attempt to overwhelm Quebec, defended by an energetic commander, with a small, ill-equipped force. Indeed, his command had been badly depleted by Montreal's occupation, bitter winter weather, and a lengthy campaign delayed by two months by the siege of St. Johns, while far from support and reinforcements. Montgomery realized that an assault had to be undertaken before the worst of winter's wrath forced a permanent end to campaigning for the season. In addition, Montgomery had little choice but to order an attack upon Quebec, before a large number of soldier enlistments expired, and before the volunteers left for home. Even worse, a smallpox epidemic sent a good many young American volunteers to early graves in the frozen grounds of the Province of Quebec, thinning the graves more than British bullets.

Ironically, as a gentleman farmer of the gentry class who farmed the land near King's Bridge, New York, and who was happily married to an attractive, vivacious wife, the retired former British officer had once expressed a strong belief in his own personal destiny by writing how, "I begin to think I shan't die by a pistol." Faced with almost insurmountable odds for success before the well-fortified city of Quebec, that earlier optimistic faith for a bright future and long life had been misplaced by the Irish general. Only recently, a more realistic General Montgomery had made out his will, as if anticipating the worst in this audacious campaign to conquer Canada with too little, and when it was already too late in winter for success. Already during the siege of Quebec, Montgomery was almost killed on December 8, when a British cannon ball decapitated the horse and destroyed his carriage just after he existed it for a conference at Colonel Arnold's headquarters: an ominous portent from a cannon's mouth.

Before the imposing fortress of Quebec, Montgomery began to realize as much. For example, he lamented to his brother-in-law, Robert Livingston, in a letter how he had no resource but to order the "storming [of] the place . . . at last." But the Irishman now wearing a blue general's uniform fully understood "the melancholy consequences" of such a desperate effort against the odds.

With time and luck running out and with harsh winter weather becoming colder, General Montgomery planned to lead his New York troops in an assault down the river road to strike the relatively weak Lower Town of Quebec from the southwest, while Arnold and his men would hit the Lower Town from the opposite direction. General Montgomery wisely concluded that it would be complete folly to assault Quebec's strong western walls, which faced the wide, open Plains of Abraham, now covered in snow, where thirty-two-year-old General James Wolfe won his climactic victory that had transformed Canada into an English possession in September 1759.

Montgomery's tactical plan called for a daring two-pronged strike that was calculated to quickly overwhelm Quebec's defenders of the Lower Town, catching them by surprise. However, a disgruntled American deserter had already warned Carleton of an impending assault. And dividing the already small American Army into two main attack columns, consisting of less than 1,000 men--to strike the Lower Town from opposite sides was a risky gamble, and a potential recipe for disaster, for if one of the columns was repulsed, dooming the other to failure.

But to enhance his slim chances for success, General Montgomery had cleverly employed two diversionary feints to mask the main point of attack, the vulnerable Lower Town, which was the key to capturing the walled Upper Town. One feint was directed at the powerful western walls looming before the sprawling Plains of Abraham. Montgomery's tactical plan meant that he had his small band of soldiers divided in four separate groups in the hope of creating maximum confusion among the British defenders, when hit from multiple directions.

Meanwhile, Montgomery prepared to strike the Lower Town from the south with his New York troops, who hopefully would unite with Arnold's column in near center of the Lower Town, before continuing on to gain the Upper Town. Montgomery also enhanced the odds for success by choosing a blinding snowstorm on December 31's night as the most opportune time to launch an assault in the hope of catching the British by surprise. Montgomery was making every effort to reverse a seemingly impossible, no-win situation by way of combining boldness with innovative tactics. But what Montgomery did not realize was that Sir Carleton had anticipated that the main strike would be directed at the Lower Town. Therefore, this experienced commander had focused his efforts on strengthening the Lower Town's defensive arrangements and preparing for the American attack.

In the snowy darkness and biting cold that would disguise the attack to maximize the chances of catching Quebec's defenders by surprise, General Montgomery and Colonel Arnold led their respective assault columns in the early morning blackness of December 31. Montgomery was determined to set the example by leading the way to inspire his soldiers forward to meet their greatest challenge to date. Under the veil of the blinding snowstorm, everything went according to Montgomery's plan in the darkness and during the early morning hours before the first light of dawn.

To reach the heart of the Lower Town from the north, Arnold's column pushed down a twisting, narrow cobblestone street–the Sault au Matelot–, which was well-defended by two barricades supported by well-placed artillery pieces. Worse of all in tactical terms, Carleton was not deceived by Montgomery's clever feints. Therefore, the Lower Town defenders were ready and waiting for the slowly advancing Americans, who were about to walk into little more than an ambush. Likewise compromising chances for success, a band of 100 Canadians who had joined the Americans deserted in the darkness, vanishing like the idealistic dream of the Fourteenth Colony. As each hour passed in the cold darkness, Montgomery's prospects for success dwindled more.

Even before the first shot was fired in the night, Colonel Arnold's situation became serious. Already the brisk snowstorm had dampened the powder, ensuring that the majority of the muskets of Arnold's troops could not be fired once the battle erupted. Nevertheless, the feisty Arnold was not deterred, and continued to lead his soldiers forward into the howling snowstorm. All of a suddenly, all hell broke loose. While at the head of his 600-man attack column striking from the north, Arnold was cut down with a nasty leg wound. Other American attackers were felled in a hail of musketry pouring from the first defensive barrier that protected the Lower Town, after passing the Palace Gate. Hit at point-blank range, Colonel Arnold's column faltered in the snow, until the capable Daniel Morgan took over.

With typical Celtic defiance and never-say-die attitude, the Ireland-born Morgan refused to forsake the desperate effort to capture Quebec, despite the ever-dwindling chances for success. Amid the blinding snowstorm swept by stiff winter wind sweeping down from the Arctic and off the St. Lawrence, the ill-clad Virginia frontiersman, a hard-bitten French and Indian War veteran and expert Indian fighter, encouraged the survivors forward through the drifting snow to resume the offensive effort. With the bulky frontiersmen Morgan leading the way as if yet battling Indians on the Virginia frontier, the cold-numbered Americans followed their Ireland-born commander. Against the odds and with a rush and a cheer, Morgan's men then overwhelmed the first defensive barrier, before moving on toward the heart of the Lower Town to exploit their success.

Meanwhile, after a torturous approach and now likewise constricted along the narrow roadway covered in snow and ice and ignoring his own portent of personal impending doom, General Montgomery led his small band of around 300 troops of the First New York Regiment toward a strong two-story blockhouse, bolstered by four 3-pounder cannon and guarding the entry point into the Lower Town, from the opposite direction as Arnold's column. Illuminating the snow-covered landscape, the first faint light of early morning revealed this formidable defensive obstacle, a two-story blockhouse, standing like a rock along his route of approach to the heart of the Lower Town.

Knowing that it was now or never, the Irish general realized that this was the key turning point of the struggle for the possession of Quebec. He, therefore, ordered a charge of his 50-man advance guard on the blockhouse at Point Diamond. As was customary, Montgomery was not only in the advance guard with his men, but also led the attack himself like an ancient Irish king of centuries past.

The relative handful of Americans, wrapped in blankets and looking more like scarecrows than soldiers, surged through the swirling snow, while General Montgomery led a mere handful of determined soldiers–four officers and thirteen men–toward a barricade and a large wooden blockhouse. They made it safely through the first barricade, and then continued onward through the snow. General Montgomery had just raised his sword and cheered his men onward, when the defenders opened up. An explosion of cannon-fire and musketry suddenly exploded from the two-story blockhouse, after the British defenders had allowed the ghost-like figures struggling through the snow to get as close as possible to inflict the maximum damage.

In the forefront as usual and wearing his trademark fur cap, General Montgomery was killed instantly when grapeshot struck him in the head and thighs. As fate would have it, Montgomery fell like a stone, never knowing what hit him. Other Irishmen, like John Captain MacPherson who was Montgomery's reliable aid-de-camp, fell in the snow. In only a matter of seconds, the audacious attack of Montgomery's band fell apart with the Irish general's death. Montgomery's discouraged soldiers withdrew back through the drifting snow and howling wind. Another Celtic officer, Colonel Donald Campbell, took command of the survivors.

Upon mutual agreement, the disheartened Americans retired, leaving Montgomery's body, along with two of his dead aides, where they had fallen in the snow. Some American wounded would freeze to death before the first light of day. Montgomery's young aid, Captain Aaron Burr, had attempted to retrieve the Irish general's body amid a hail of bullets. But Burr, a Princeton graduate of promise, had been unable to bring his beloved commander's body through the deep snow and off the field.

Meanwhile, Colonel Arnold's column was left to fight alone for possession of Quebec, and would shortly be overpowered by overwhelming numbers. Ironically, a good many Irish in redcoats were now destined to save Quebec and Canada from conquest. All in all, the American bid to capture Quebec was quickly turning into a disaster, after the fall of the two dynamic commanders, Montgomery and Arnold. But by far the most damaging blow to the overall offensive effort was Montgomery's death, which resulted in his column's repulse in the driving snow.

Other Irish soldiers besides General Montgomery and Captain MacPherson fell to rise no more during the nightmare of what had become an ice and snow battle in Quebec's windy, bullet-swept streets. A member of Captain Thayer's company of Rhode Islanders, Irishman Patrick Tracy was killed in the doomed assault on Quebec. Two other Irish soldiers of Captain Thayer's company fell wounded amid the icy winds sweeping off the icy St. Lawrence, Corporal James Hayden and Private Cornelius Hagerty. One day in the near future in honor of the fallen General Montgomery, Captain Thayer would name his next son, Richard Montgomery Thayer.

Meanwhile, after Montgomery's death, the Ireland-born Morgan led his boys onward. They surged farther down the snowy Sault au Matelot and assaulted the second defensive barrier of stone walls that towered a dozen feet high on the frozen landscape like a medieval castle. Consequently, the Irishman's success resulted in large numbers of dazed prisoners, encumbering his offensive operations. Hesitant, more conservative top lieutenants now convinced the hard-fighting Irishman to concentrate his scattered forces to wait the arrival of Montgomery's column—which was not coming—, before continuing onward to capitalize on Morgan's tactical gains. For one of the few times in his life, Morgan relented. However, the Irishman soon regretted his decision of not continuing the attack toward the center of the Lower Town. As he later wrote: "To these arguments I sacrificed my own opinion and lost the town" of Quebec.

Indeed, Morgan and his soldiers had lost the initiative at

the second barricade. Now the bitter end of the efforts of the Northern Department Army to capture Quebec was only a matter of time. Indeed, the British defenders had not only concentrated at the second barrier but were reinforced by newly arriving troops who poured through the Palace Gate and smashed into the vulnerable rear of what little was left of Morgan's column.

Capitulation was now the only alternative for the hard-fighting Irishman, despite having plenty of old scores to settle with the British, including nearly 500 lashes inflicted upon his back as punishment during the French and Indian War. At around 9:00 a.m. in the snowy hell of Quebec's icy streets and with no alternative remaining, Morgan and his band finally surrendered. Of the around 800 American attackers, nearly 500 were killed, wounded, or captured in the fiasco. America's ill-fated bid to capture Quebec and make Canada the fourteenth colony had become a debacle of the first order.

After the repulse of the two primary American columns and the battle's close, General Montgomery's body was found by the British victors in a snow drift. Mercifully, he had been killed instantly, sparing him the agony of freezing to death like other American wounded. Because the Irishman had been a distinguished and most promising officer in Great Britain's armies for so many years, General Montgomery's remains was treated with a rare measure of reverence and respect for a "rebel," who fought against the King. As a cruel fate would have it, this gifted Irish general from New York became the most senior Continental officer killed in action during the American Revolution.

Tragically, when killed on December 31's morning, General Montgomery never learned of his well-deserved promotion to major general for his capture of Montreal and other successes during the Canadian campaign of 1775. Indeed, Montgomery had accomplished a great deal before his untimely death, capturing most of inhabited Canada along the St. Lawrence and the key city of Montreal, winning the first two victories of the Continental Army.

One important consequence of General Montgomery's death on Quebec's streets was the Continental Congress' belated decision to embark immediately upon the professionalization of the American military. By this measure, it was hoped that no longer would short-time soldier enlistments would sabotage overall strategy, such as Montgomery's premature order to assault on Quebec out of urgent necessity, because enlistments were about to expire at year's end. Thereafter, the Continental Congress began to enlist troops for years instead of months to create an experienced cadre of Continental troops, or regulars, who served as the backbone of Washington's Army: a key requirement for winning a lengthy war of attrition.

Additionally, General Montgomery's death gave the infant American nation its first martyr and hero of the war. Public mourning and memorials across the thirteen colonies were dedicated to the memory of the lamented General Montgomery, who also became America's most grieved Irish martyr of the American Revolution. For instance, the esteemed author of *Common Sense*, Thomas Paine, wrote a popular pamphlet entitled, *A Dialogue between the Ghost of General Montgomery Just Arrived from the Elysian Fields.* The new American nation successfully employed General Montgomery's heroic example to fuel patriotism and enlistments across the thirteen colonies. And no Americans were more inspired to avenge the loss of this promising Ireland-born general than the Irish and Scotch-Irish, who flocked to the ranks in large numbers after General Montgomery's death at Quebec.

In this inspirational way, Montgomery's legacy continued to live on long after his death, and the overly-optimistic Congressional members and military leaders yet dreamed of

28

conquering Canada. In early 1776, the Continental Congress sent four commissioners, including seventy-year-old Benjamin Franklin, on a diplomatic mission to solicit French Canadian support and aid for the defeated American Army that remained in Canada. Two commissioners were Irish Catholics, Charles Carroll of Carrollton and his cousin Reverend John Carroll, who was a Jesuit priest and the future Archbishop of Baltimore, Maryland. The commissioners' mission was to exploit the nationalism of the French Canadian Catholics and rally support against the British. In overall terms, the Catholic and Jesuit connection represented a politically astute bid by Congress, or more specifically John Adams, to gain sympathy and support from the Catholic French Canadians for American independence. However, influential priests had thoroughly convinced the French Canadians that the Protestant Americans would persecute them for their Catholicism, if they united with their former enemies of the French and Indian War.

One central objective of this key diplomatic mission was to attempt to convince the Archbishop of Quebec to repeal the decision to ex-communicate any French Canadian, who assisted the Americans in their bid to conquer Canada in the hope that more French Canadians would assist the American Army in its bid to transform Canada into the Fourteenth Colony.

Arriving with reinforcements from Pennsylvania, General John Sullivan, the son of two hardy Irish migrants and lawyer from New Hampshire, took command of the American army in Canada in the hope of yet conquering Canada in early June 1776. While the ever-ambitious Continental Congress continued to dream of the addition of a Fourteenth Colony, that legislative body and the infant republic now counted upon the military abilities of other Irish soldiers, such as Colonel William Maxwell, Colonel William Thompson, and Colonel William Irvine, who were all born in Ireland, while

Colonel Anthony Wayne descended from Irish parents from northern Ireland.

Obeying the Continental Congress' wishes, Washington had only reluctantly dispatched some of America's "best men," who served in largely Irish and Scotch-Irish regiments of the Pennsylvania Line, to reinforce the Continental Army in Canada. This timely reinforcement included four regiments, commanded by Irish commanders, Colonel Thompson who led the First Pennsylvania Regiment, Colonel John Shee who commanded the Fourth Pennsylvania Regiment, and Colonel Irvine, who headed the Sixth Pennsylvania Regiment. The campaign to capture Quebec, under the supervision of General Sullivan, finally ended in the late spring of 1776, with the arrival of thousands of British reinforcements and disaster for the American invaders at Trois Rivieres on the St. Lawrence and about halfway between Montreal and Quebec. Both Ireland-born generals, Irvine and Thompson, were captured during the fiasco along with a good many of their Irish and Scotch-Irish troops from Pennsylvania.

Even more than the Trois Rivieres defeat, Montgomery's death at Quebec on 1775's final day continued to be lamented across the thirteen colonies long thereafter, because no other American commander seemingly possessed a comparable military ability, or had been blessed with so much potential as this dynamic Irishman. For instance, the brilliant John Adams wrote how, "Since the Death of Montgomery, We have had no General in Command [in Canada] who Seems" able to match General Montgomery in ability and skill.

In 1828 and thirteen years after his great War of 1812 victory over a powerful invading British Army at New Orleans, Louisiana, another Ireland-born soldier and a revolutionary war veteran, Andrew Jackson, wrote with admiration about a fellow countryman, who became one of his heroes: "the patriotic Genl. Montgomery, who will ever live in the hearts of his countrymen" from Ireland.

Indeed, in almost accomplishing the impossible against the odds, General Montgomery "was only a few hundred yards away from conquering Canada" and capturing the capital of all Canada, Quebec, and from adding a Fourteenth Colony to a new American nation born in violent revolution. Even though British soldiers had buried the body of Montgomery, the conqueror of Montreal, in a solemn ceremony and with full military honors in a tribute, they could not bury Montgomery's contributions or enduring legacy. The Irishman's audacious invasion of Canada was destined to have a significant overall strategic impact on the course of the American Revolution. Historian Thomas J. Fleming emphasized how the invasion of Canada played a key role in convincing the French to "decide that secret intervention might be worth at try" in America, helping to pave the way to the invaluable 1778 French Alliance that was crucial for the winning of the American Revolution.

Chapter II: Irish and Scotch-Irish from Maryland and Delaware Accomplishing the Impossible at the Battle of Long Island, August 27, 1776

Mirroring the realities of commercial life in the city of Philadelphia, many leading merchants and businessmen of the busy port of Baltimore, Maryland, were Irish. These transplanted Irish had played early key roles in the development of the once sleepy port village, that mushroomed during the American Revolution, on the Patapsco River, which connected to the Chesapeake Bay. Thanks to the booming commercial trade, these enterprising Emerald Islanders helped to transform Baltimore into a thriving trading port city.

However, compared to Philadelphia that was America's largest city during the colonial period, Baltimore was yet a young, small town by the time of the American Revolution's beginning. Nevertheless, Baltimore possessed seemingly limitless potential, thanks to its strategic location near Chesapeake Bay's head. Symbolically, many Irish merchants of Baltimore and other American ports were recent Emerald Isle immigrants, after having been "driven from Ireland by England's unjust tariff laws [and] These men hated England" and possessed plenty of scores to settle with the detested King. What had happened to these Irishmen and their families for generations on the Green Isle ensured an unflinching support for the patriot cause by 1775.

Long before the American Revolution's outbreak, the fertile lands of western Maryland, with its abundant cheap land and natural beauty, was a remote frontier that beckoned Irish and Scotch-Irish settlers like a magnet. By the thousands, Irish and Scotch-Irish migrants flocked to the western Maryland frontier, including the fertile valley of the Monocacy River just on the east side of the Appalachian Mountains, to start life anew.

Thousands of acres in this fertile region along the chocolate-colored Monocacy were owned by Charles Carroll, a second generation Irishman. He was destined to become a leader revolutionary and signer of the Declaration of Independence. By the time of the American Revolution, he was one of the leading citizens of the bustling port of Annapolis, Maryland, on the Chesapeake. By the early 1730s, Carroll owned 10,000 acres nestled in the rich lands located between the Potomac and Monocacy Rivers, near where the two rivers intersected, called Carrollton. This fertile region was largely settled by Irish immigrants, who made their dreams come true in this new land. Here, on the Carroll estate in this new "Canaan" of western Maryland, these hard-working Irish immigrants, both free small farmers and tenant farmers, helped to clear a wilderness area and tame the land.

Ironically, in utilizing tenant farmers from Ireland, Carroll, a devout Catholic who yet embraced a love for old Ireland, differed from most other Maryland landowners, who improved their lands principally by slave labor. The memory of the loss of ancestral family wealth and lands in Ireland to the British conquers reminded Carroll to attempt to do whatever he could to help the miserable plight of the Irish people. The legacy of Ireland's past guaranteed that he would long promote the future settlement of his fellow Irish countrymen across the Maryland frontier.

By the 1750s, around 16,000-17,000 of Maryland's population, of an estimated 160,000, were members of the Catholic faith. Like the nearby colony of Pennsylvania, Maryland especially welcomed Irish Catholics from the beginning, having been originally established as a Catholic colony. Baltimore would eventually become the center of Catholicism in America, thanks largely to its solid colonial antecedents. The vast majority of the Irish Catholic settlers were small farmers, but a Catholic gentry class also developed in Maryland. By the time of the American Revolution, Charles Carroll was among the richest Catholics in all of Maryland. He became one of the principal Maryland Catholic leaders by the time of the showdown between the thirteen colonies and the Mother Country.

Having learned the bitter lessons from the Emerald Isle past, Irish Catholics across Maryland became increasingly concerned about the increase in Protestant power by the late 1600s. Ironically, this development helped to lay yet another foundation for these disenfranchised Irish Catholics to resort to open revolt against the strongest Protestant nation on earth, England. In 1744, the council of Maryland, composed of leading Protestants, ordered that Maryland Catholics could no longer enlist in the militia, because of spreading fear resulting from the Jacobite rebellions in Scotland and England and the stereotypical Protestant belief, on both sides of the Atlantic, that the most dangerous of all were "his Majesty's Roman Catholick [sic] Subjects." In addition, Irish Catholics were not allowed to hold public office in Maryland.

Such discriminatory anti-Catholic legislative acts passed in Maryland reminded the Irish of Maryland, especially recent immigrants, of the Penal Codes of Ireland. Constructed in Machiavellian fashion by Ireland's conquers, these discriminatory codes had systematically stripped the Irish Catholics of their personal rights and liberties, ensuring widespread oppression and persecution against Irish Catholics in their own native homeland. During the colonial period, an all-consuming fear persisted among Maryland's Irish Catholics about the possible passage of new laws at anytime by Protestant colonial rulers, who would then systematically erode their wealth and land-holdings, as in Ireland.

What ultimately healed ancient wounds and finally more closely united Maryland Catholics and Protestants was both the frontier experience and the Indian threat stemming from the French and Indian Wars. This common Indian and French threat united American colonists of all faiths out of the need for mutual survival against a powerful foe on the western frontier.

Like the earlier Native American threat, the call to arms against the British in 1775 also united both Irish Catholics and Scotch Irish Protestants to defend the land that they loved. Learning of the unprecedented accuracy and long-range capabilities of the frontier long rifle that was unknown in the northern colonies, Congress voted in mid-June 1775 to organize ten companies of "expert riflemen" from the western frontier regions of Pennsylvania (six companies), Virginia (two companies), and Maryland (two companies).

These two Maryland rifle companies of frontiersmen from the wilds of western Maryland were led by Captain Thomas Price and Captain Michael Cresap. An explorer of the Ohio country on the west side of the mountains, Cresap was a frontier commander who excelled at Indian fighting in the wilderness. He possessed ample experience as a captain of militia. Cresap was the son of the most legendary frontiersmen of western Maryland, Colonel Thomas Cresap. Michael's father was known far and wide as the "Rattlesnake Colonel," because of his combative nature and feisty spirit in opposition to all enemies, Indians, French, Canadians, Pennsylvanians, or the British themselves.

Confident of success, the hardy frontiersmen of these two frontier companies departed the small western Maryland town of Frederick at the foot of the heavily-forested mountains, while "painted like Indians, armed with tomahawks and rifles, dressed in hunting-shirts and moccasins." Meanwhile, with the call to arms, the mustering of additional troops across Maryland continued unabated. One of Baltimore's son who answered the call was Samuel Smith. He hailed from one of the leading merchant families of Baltimore, Samuel Smith, who was born in County Tyrone, Ireland. Like so many other Irish and Scotch-Irish, Smith migrated to the wilds of Pennsylvania and settled in that colony the 1720s, before migrating farther west to the frontier village of Carlisle, Pennsylvania, around 1750.

However, the hard-hitting Indian raids along the western Pennsylvania frontier forced the Smith family to join the exodus of panicked settlers fleeing eastward to escape the threat. In 1760, the Smith family then relocated to the safety of Baltimore. Here, John Smith, Samuel's father, became a leading merchant of the bustling port city. In time and after receiving his education at the Elkton, Maryland, academy and after joining his father's business at age fifteen, Samuel became one of Baltimore's wealthiest merchants.

Samuel Smith also became of the primary revolutionary leaders of Baltimore. He early took a stand against arbitrary British authority and dictatorial powers like so many people of Baltimore. John Smith served on the Committee of Correspondence and Committee of Observation. His son, Samuel Smith, who was named in honor of his Irish grandfather, had been recently engaged in securing business clients for his family's mercantile firm, John Smith & Sons, all across Europe and Mediterranean region. Samuel was mature at only age twenty two, shouldering multiple responsibilities with ease. As soon as serious trouble developed between the thirteen colonies and Great Britain, the prosperous mercantile firm of John Smith & Sons began to trade wheat and flour for ammunition and weapons to supply patriot troops for the upcoming conflict.

As a proud member of Baltimore's social elite and one of the port city's most promising sons, Samuel Smith served as a member of the Baltimore Independent Cadets. This volunteer company was known as the elite militia unit of the city. Demonstrating leadership ability, Smith soon rose to

the rank of sergeant. He then became the adjutant of the
Baltimore Independent Cadets, filling an officer's position of
responsibility. The military experience gained by Smith with
the Baltimore Independent Cadets, consisting of Baltimore's
best and brightest sons, led to his election as a company
commander in Colonel William Smallwood's Battalion of
Continental infantry in early 1776.

Utilizing his expertise, he vigorously trained not only
his own Baltimore company but also two other companies of
Colonel Smallwood's Battalion at Baltimore during the
winter of 1775-1776. Captain Smith was destined to
become "one of the ablest officers in the army" of General
Washington. Colonel Smallwood, a genteel Maryland
gentleman tobacco farmer with solid militia experience and a
pious bachelor of the Episcopalian faith, possessed a trusty
company commander in the versatile Captain Smith.

For the most part, Colonel Smallwood "recruited many
Irishmen for his [Maryland battalion and at] least one-half of
Smallwood's men were Irish or of Irish descent." Indeed,
this fine, well-trained Continental battalion was "composed
of the flower of Maryland youth, both Catholic and
Protestant [and it was destined to become] the Tenth Legion
[or Julius Caesar's famed Legion] of the American Army"
throughout the long years of the American Revolution.

Many of Colonel Smallwood's troops hailed from the
largely Catholic counties of southern Maryland, where fertile
tobacco farms and plantations were spread across the gently
rolling, fertile lands nestled between the Potomac River and
the Chesapeake Bay. This was Smallwood's native
homeland, and a source of pride. He had been born in 1732
in Charles County, Maryland. Smallwood's sprawling
tobacco plantation, named Mattawoman, bordered the east
bank of the Potomac River in Charles County, and the salty,
brownish-hued tidewater estuary known as Mattawoman
Creek. Even by the American Revolution's beginning, this

picturesque region was yet a virgin land distinguished by rolling hills, virgin hardwood forests, Magnolia swamps, and rich, dark soil that produced bountiful yields of tobacco.

The busy port of Baltimore contributed many excellent troops, like Captain Samuel Smith, to the ranks of Colonel Smallwood's Battalion, both officers and enlisted men. But the most distinguished of these young men of promise was Mordecai Gist. He was a Baltimore merchant who was placed in charge of American forces in Baltimore. Born in Maryland in 1742, he had organized the first volunteer infantry company from Maryland in 1774, the Baltimore Independent Cadets. Well-disciplined and trained, the Baltimore Independent Cadets served as the reliable core unit for Colonel Smallwood's Battalion, providing an elite cadre of disciplined officers and men. Not surprisingly, therefore, Gist was soon destined for a high rank in Colonel Smallwood's Battalion, and a well-deserved reputation as a fine commander and a resourceful fighter.

The companies of Colonel Smallwood's Battalion of Maryland Continentals that had been organized in 1776's spring at the ports of Annapolis and Baltimore consisted of more than five hundred zealous young volunteers. With Colonel Smallwood leading the way, the Continentals of the Maryland Battalion marched north on a nearly 600-mile journey to join General Washington's Army at New York City in July 1776, not long after learning of the Declaration of Independence's signing on July 4. Attempting to reach the fledgling Continental Army before it was too late to meet the anticipated British invasion, the Marylanders' rapid push north through the hot summer weather and along the dusty roads was so arduous that young Captain Cresap became so ill from exhaustion and sickness that he soon died.

Like most units of the revolutionary army, Smallwood's Maryland Battalion of Continental troops was commanded by some leading political figures of Maryland. On January 1,

1776, when the Maryland Convention voted to establish regular units that led to the creation of Smallwood's Battalion, influential members of this convention included William Smallwood, Lieutenant Colonel Francis Ware, and four captains, who became leading officers of this new battalion of Continental troops from Maryland. The seven companies of the Maryland Battalion that reached New York City and Washington's Army in early August 1776 combined with the two companies from the western Maryland frontier, which was heavily populated with Irish and Scotch-Irish like those units from the Pennsylvania and Virginia frontiers.

Consequently, in total, Colonel Smallwood commanded nine companies, which were led, from the First Company to the Ninth Company; by Captains John Hoskins Stone, William Hyde, Barton Lucas, Thomas Ewing, Nathaniel Ramsay, Peter Adams, John Day Scott, Samuel Smith, and George Stricker. Born in 1741 and a 1767 graduate of Princeton College, Captain Ramsay was the son of an Irish immigrant from the Province of Ulster, northern Ireland. The Maryland Battalion's strength peaked at around 750 soldiers. Many of these men were either Irish Catholics or Irish Presbyterians who served together as the cause of independence transcended religious differences. After demonstrating leadership ability and promise, Thomas Price and Mordecai Gist were promoted to the rank of major, serving as Colonel Smallwood's reliable top lieutenants.

By the late summer of 1776, the fate of the American war effort hung in the balance with the fast-approaching showdown for possession of New York City between General Washington's Army and the largest British fleet and most powerful British Army ever dispatched to America. The novice commander-in-chief had committed the cardinal sin of having divided his army by attempting to defend too much territory with too few troops against the most powerful British force were ever placed into the field. Over-optimistic in terms of his tactical thinking and abiding by Congress' dictates, General Washington hoped to retain possession of both New York City and Long Island. But such an ambitious objective was a strategic and tactical impossibility given not only the presence of the large British Army but also the vast British Navy that controlled the waterways that surrounded the city and Manhattan Island.

Consequently, Washington possessed little, if any, realistic chance of successfully defending New York City during 1776's summer. The bulk of Washington's Army, around 9,000 men who lacked experience and training, were positioned on Long Island, while 7,000 troops held Manhattan Island, and another 4,000 soldiers were scattered in defensive positions in New Jersey on the west side of the Hudson River. The strategic bone of contention was now America's most strategic city, New York.

Clearly, Washington and his army were in a precarious position by the late summer of 1776, after the inexperienced Virginia commander-in-chief had split most of his army in two to defend both Long Island and Manhattan Island. Now the American forces were divided by the wide mouth of the Hudson River, separating Manhattan Island from Long Island, at a time when the British Navy controlled both the seas and the maze of waterways around New York City. The arrival of the immense British fleet at the end of June 1776 caused Ireland-born Colonel Edward Hand, commanding the advanced American outpost on Long Island near Denyse Point and in charge of the band of Pennsylvania soldiers patrolling the Long Island shore, to warn Washington and write a letter to his beloved wife Kitty, who had recently visited the army: "I am very happy that you are now out of the way of Hurry [because] a Fleet of upwards of 100 Sail of Different Burthens arrived . . . yesterday [and] we can't make a stand here alone if they think proper to land any number [on Long Island], we have prepared everything for retreat to the main Body . . . ."

While Colonel Hand warned Washington that the British were about to disembark from Staten Island, just south of Manhattan Island, and descend upon Long Island in force after pushing east to cross the watery pass known as the Narrows, General Washington was yet unsure if these highly professional soldiers planned to unleash their main effort on Long Island, or if all that British activity was only a clever feint. Despite Hand's warnings by both written messages and signal flags from the point on Long Island closest to Staten Island, Washington was badly mistaken in not believing that the greatest threat would be directed at Long Island, and that his men would soon be in jeopardy. All in all, Washington's tactical situation–a classic case of divide and conquer--on Long Island was a recipe for disaster for the novice commander-in-chief and an untrained American army yet to receive its baptismal fire.

On August 27, General William Howe prepared to deliver a death blow to the largest concentration of American troops, who were isolated and vulnerable on Long Island. After a successful amphibious landing on the western end of Long Island, adjacent to Staten Island and south of Brooklyn, at Denyse Point, thousands of General Howe's troops poured inland like a flood. Moving ashore with confidence, the foremost British troops met little opposition. Around 17,000 well-equipped British and Hessian soldiers, who possessed plenty of military experience and discipline unlike the 9,000 amateur American soldiers on Long Island, launched an offensive calculated to end the upstart American rebellion in one stroke.

Meanwhile, thousands of British and Hessian soldiers pushed deeper into the lowland plain of the southwestern end of Long Island, expanding their beachhead farther inland. Ironically, the only acts of defiance coming from the Americans on Long Island developed from the lone Irish

41

colonel and his small command of riflemen of the First
Pennsylvania Continental Regiment, Hand. Wisely, Hand
had decided not to make a stand along the beach to confront
the amphibious landing, or his command would have been
wiped out.

Forced to withdraw from Denyse Point as the British
swarmed inland like a locust plague, the ever-dependable
Hand and a few hundred of his largely Scotch-Irish
Continental solders from Pennsylvania then burned supplies
and foodstuffs, especially bushels of wheat, and whatever the
invading British and Hessians could utilize in their invasion.
After harassing the left flank of Lord Cornwallis troops and
destroying what the British needed both for themselves and
their horses, Hand withdrew to the forested terrain around
the high ground of Prospect Hill just north of the village of
Flatbush, after the British and Hessians pushed northeast
from Gravesend Bay to reach Flatbush.

Against the odds, the resourceful Irish colonel, who was
a former British officer, now commanding this crack
Pennsylvania rifle regiment knew well how to fight an
advancing opponent either in the open field or in delaying
actions. Most important, Hand understood the value of a
scorched earth policy and how detrimentally it could affect
an invader's movements and psychology. With tens of
thousands of British and Hessian soldiers now on Long
Island, Colonel Hand might have wondered if he would ever
again see his pretty wife or his new baby girl, Sarah, who he
fondly called "little Sally." Most important, the reliance of
Washington, who was at this Manhattan Island headquarters,
on Hand's intelligence of British movements on Long Island
was complete by this time.

However, the Irish colonel was not about to give up or
relinquish ground anymore without a fight. Colonel Hand
made preparations to launch a bold night attack from the
thick woodlands of Flatbush Pass in the darkness of August

22-23 to catch the Hessian pickets and sentries just north of Cornwallis' encampment in and around the small Dutch village of Flatbush by surprise. He hoped to slow the advance inland and buy precious time or American troops to adjust tactically to meet the crisis. Hand's nighttime attack with around 550 First Pennsylvania Continentals surprised the Hessians, causing consternation. But the Germans eventually rallied and brought artillery into bear on the Pennsylvania riflemen. A combination of strong resistance and confusion in the blackness forced Colonel Hand to call off his audacious strike. But most important in purely psychological terms, Hand and his mostly Irish and Scotch-Irish soldiers had struck the first blow at the enemy on Long Island, alerting Lord Cornwallis that he faced an unpredictable opponent.

Despite not reaping a more impressive tactical success, Hand was not yet finished, however. On the hot afternoon of August 23, the determined Irishman attacked once more. He had earlier struck the German mercenaries and caught them by surprise at night. Now he would try to hit the invaders in broad daylight when they least expected. Therefore, Hand and his mostly Pennsylvania Scotch-Irish smashed into the foremost Hessian outpost, hurling the most advanced Germans rearward. Shocked by the Irishman's attack, the Hessians retreated to rejoin their main body of Cornwallis' troops at Flatbush. Some house-to-house fighting took place when the Pennsylvanians reached the village. Hand's Pennsylvanians even burned houses that offered shelter to the Hessians. Recovering from their surprise, a German counterattack ended the threat so unexpectedly posed by Hand, who then retired to their high ground, timbered perch around Flatbush Pass.

Thereafter, Hand continued to harass the enemy, as if refusing to acknowledge that the British and Hessians had gained a permanent toehold on Long Island. He ordered his

Pennsylvania riflemen, who were expert marksmen with the long rifle, to concentrate on harassing the pinned-down Hessian troops in and around Flatbush. The accurate fire of Hand's boys, in frontier-style hunting shirts and carrying tomahawks, was effective, infuriating the Germans who were only familiar with fighting in the open European-style without ever facing the long rifle's wrath. Irish and Scotch-Irish frontiersmen firing from behind trees and houses was a new kind of warfare to these young German mercenaries so far from home. For the Hessians, this encounter was their first experience with the American way of war, and Colonel Hand became a master of these guerrilla-style tactics. For instance, Hand once again attacked the Hessian encampment on the night of August 26, causing havoc. Brisk firing and Indian-like war-cries from the distant frontier pierced the darkness, awaking the startled Hessians at 2 o'clock a.m., after having caught them by surprise once again.

But neither Hand or Washington could image the next tactical move about to be undertaken by General Howe. A bold, imaginative tactical plan was adopted by the British to ensure victory on Long Island: a flank march northeastward was conducted by the main body of British troops and south of the American defenses. Howe's soldiers swung below the American defensive lines, which ran along the high ground of Brooklyn Heights that ran east-west across Long Island. This stealthy flank march of 10,000 British troops of the right wing under General George Clinton successfully bypassed the American defenses on the east, after easing through a wide-open Jamaica Pass, left undefended by colonial troops, that cut through the heights.

Ironically, much like the battle of Gettysburg, Pennsylvania, during the Civil War, the "largest battle of the American Revolution was set in motion [on the evening of August 26] by an unexpected encounter in a watermelon patch," in the words of author Barnet Schecter. At that time, a 5,000-man column under General James Grant, on the British left, or westernmost, flank, was moving forward and up the Gowanus Road in order to distract Colonel Hand from giving warning of the stealthy flank march of the British right wing through Jamaica Pass. During the night along the march up the Gowanus Road and just before midnight, the British advance guard discovered a patch of ripe watermelons–"an American delicacy"–near Red Lion Inn, which was located directly south of Gowanus Bay. The Hungry Britons then raided the melon patch, until Hand's riflemen opened fire to initiate the battle of Long Island, before retiring northward before the British advance in the inky blackness. So far, Colonel Hand and his Pennsylvania boys, acting as an independent command as if serving on the western frontier, had done a fine job. The reliable soldiers of Hand's First Continental Regiment not only harassed the enemy, but also observed and gathered intelligence for four days with respite or relief.

But to the east on the British right wing, far more important tactical developments than a spirited clash in a watermelon patch were about to take place. With the unprotected American left flank, under General Sullivan, hanging vulnerable in mid-air, thanks to the tactical shortcomings of the decision-making of an inexperienced American leadership, Lord Stirling, on the far right on the southernmost end of the American line, was alerted by General Israel Putnam about the growing threat around 3 o'clock on August 27's sweltering morning. Lord Stirling, or William Alexander of the Alexander clan of the Scottish lowlands and from a leading New York City family, was ordered to assemble as many available American troops as possible to meet the threat. The high-spirited Celtic commander was ordered to march south to stop General James Grant's advance north pouring up the Gowanus Road. General Grant's troops of the British Army's left wing advanced steadily toward not only the southernmost, but also the westernmost position of the American lines.

To achieve his objective to somehow halt the advance of General Grant's 5,000-man column surging northward, Lord Stirling would depend primarily upon two crack units to serve as a sturdy foundation for his brigade's defensive stand against the odds, even though neither command were of regimental size or full strength by this time: a Continental battalion of Delaware troops and six companies of the Maryland Battalion. Smallwood's Maryland Battalion had dwindled from 400 to around 300 soldiers, including key officers like Captain Cresap, from the ravages of disease in August alone.

Like Colonel Smallwood's Marylanders, the Delaware Continentals were good troops that could be counted upon in a crisis, despite their relative inexperience. Fortunately, for American fortunes today, vigorous training and drill compensated in part for the inexperience of both the Marylanders and Delaware troops, however. From the lower counties of Delaware, this fine battalion of Delaware Continentals had been organized in January 1776. Tough and dependable, this unit consisted of eight companies from New Castle, Sussex, and Kent Counties, Delaware. Worthy Celtic compatriots of the Maryland Irish and much like the ethnic composition of the Maryland Battalion, this Delaware unit was "composed largely of Irishmen" from the three lower counties along the Delaware River.

Not only considerably reduced in strength, the Maryland Battalion was also without its esteemed commander, Colonel Smallwood. Ironically, with America's most important battle to date imminent, the southern Marylander now sat on court martial duty in New York City. But the Maryland soldiers were fortunate to have a most worthy replacement in Major Mordecai Gist. He was blessed with not only a Biblical first name, but also a feisty spirit and penchant for hard fighting. Thanks to fate and circumstance, this promising young officer from Baltimore's cobblestone streets was destined to take the colonel's place on the day of destiny on Long Island.

Ironically, the Delaware Battalion was also now without its revered leader, Ireland-born Colonel John Haslet. He was a fighting Presbyterian reverend, who waged a holy war against the British and Hessians. When appointed commander of the Delaware Battalion, Haslet possessed solid military experience as the colonel of the Lower Regiment, Kent County Militia. He had served as a resourceful captain in the 1758 British-colonial expedition to the Ohio country in the attempt to capture Fort Duquesne during the French and Indian War. This promising Scotch-Irish colonel of ability now served on the same court martial board as Smallwood in New York City.

By this time when Long Island was the strategic key to New York City, American forces on Long Island could not have been in a more precarious position or disadvantageous tactical situation. After the stealthy flank march northeastward around the left flank of the American Army and through Jamaica Pass and then turning in the opposite direction to push west, General Howe had managed to not only out-flank the American defensive positions along the high ground of Brooklyn Heights, but also to position his forces in the rear of the American lines. Unprepared to meet the unexpected threat from the rear, the routing of the inexperienced American troops by so many trained professionals in scarlet was all but inevitable. The American left under General Sullivan, whose troops were facing the opposite, or wrong, direction, when hit by the massive British onslaught led by General Clinton.

While the American left was in serious trouble, Lord Stirling early rose to the challenge in facing the threat from the British left wing under General Grant. In the steamy half-light of early morning yet hot and humid, Stirling ordered Smallwood's and Haslet's commands forward in the raging storm. Major Gist led his Marylanders, while Major Thomas McDonough, another reliable Irish commander who now took his Ireland-born commander's place, encouraged his Delaware Continentals onward. Half a mile north of the Red Lion Inn, Stirling and his Maryland and Delaware boys found Colonel Atlee and his Pennsylvania Battalion and Connecticut troops, under Lieutenant Colonel Joel Clark, making a defensive stand. All of these troops were commanded Colonel Samuel Holden Parsons, a distinguished Harvard graduate and a clergyman's son. With flintlocks on shoulders, Atlee's Pennsylvania soldiers pushed forward in the hope of delaying the British advance to buy time for Stirling's hard-hit battle-line, or the American right flank, to yet take shape in the early morning light.

In command of his small brigade and throughout the early morning's hours, Lord Stirling battled the British left wing under General Grant with spirit. A tough British professional who had served in America during the French and Indian War, Grant kept Lord Stirling's Americans on the far right under pressure and in a stationary position as planned, while the American left was in crisis. With pressure mounting, Lord Stirling ordered his Pennsylvania skirmishers under Colonel Atlee to retire before General Grant's advance around 8 o'clock. Nevertheless, the Pennsylvania soldiers had bought precious time in delaying the British advance. To meet the growing threat, the Maryland troops of only 400 soldiers were aligned across the Gowanus, or Shore, Road on the left atop a hill in a belt of woods, while suffering a rising rate of casualties from the fire of Grant's batteries.

Meanwhile, Howe's masterful battle-plan worked to perfection: Grant's diversionary attack on the right flank drew the focus of the Americans' attention, including even dispatching reinforcements, while General Howe, who directed the main British offensive effort with 10,000 men, smashed to the colonial's other flank. As Lord Sterling's soldiers held firm to the west, Howe's troops routed Sullivan's Division to the northeast, after plowing through the American lines from the rear and gaining the left flank. During the battle of Brooklyn, or Long Island, on scorching August 27, the division of General Sullivan, the feisty New England commander who was proud of his northern Ireland roots, was decimated by the overwhelming combined might of German Hessians. Caught by surprise, hundreds of Sullivan's soldiers, including the general himself, were quickly encircled and captured. There unfortunates "were nearly all Irish" in one estimation.

Those of Sullivan's troops who had escaped the initial attack were cut-off by the British breakthrough from retreat to the safety of Manhattan Island and New York City. The last avenue open for retreat now lay across the dark waters of Gowanus Creek, that entered Gowanus Bay, and the steamy lowlands of salt marshes, salt reed meadows, and placid mill ponds located below Brooklyn heights, upon which the America inner defensive lines were perched.

After the rout of Sullivan's Division and most of Washington's ill-fated forces on Long Island, after the collapse of both the American left and center, consequently, the strategic crossroads of the Porte and Gowanus Road on the right flank, held by Lord Stirling's brigade, was crucial to hold at all costs. This key strategic position now had to be held in order to allow the escape of thousands of American survivors, victims of the rout. Here, on the right flank, this southernmost sector held by Lord Stirling was now the only American position yet standing firm on this fateful day. At one point, Atlee's Pennsylvania troops had even counterattacked to buy more time and breathing room for Stirling's men.

However, the rout left Stirling's forces in a most

precarious situation   Now victorious British troops under General Clinton and Lord Cornwallis descended southward in the attempt to overwhelm Lord Stirling's small, isolated brigade. Against the odds, Stirling's men faced south and were held in place by General Grant's increasing pressure from the south. Lord Stirling and his tiny brigade were about to be encircled by Lord Cornwallis's troops from the north, who continued to pour south toward Lord Stirling's left flank and rear. While Germans in blue uniforms were about to smash into Lord Stirling's vulnerable flank, thousands of British grenadiers rushed toward his brigade's rear.

     Worst of all, Lord Stirling and his soldiers had not yet been warned of the disaster on the American left and center. This development left Lord Stirling and his men on the right on their own. As fate would have it, only Stirling and his brigade held firm. The only possible avenue of escape was north along the dusty Gowanus Road, which was now filled with the dense ranks of advancing redcoats, and across Gowanus Creek to reach the surviving Americans of the inner line of Brooklyn Heights to the north. However, this "natural line of retreat" was now blocked by the 80 yards of brackish saltwater that was wide Gowanus Creek, spanning northeast and toward the American fortified position on Brooklyn Heights directly to the north, which entered Gowanus Bay just to the southwest.

     All the while, Major Gist's Marylanders and Major McDonough's Delaware Continental troops held firm under the pounding administered by the advancing redcoats and Hessians. In this crisis situation, only these two diminutive groups of Continentals from neighboring states anchored Lord Stirling's shattered right flank. Fortunately for the routed American army in this crisis situation, however, the 400 Maryland troops were some of the most disciplined and reliable in the army.

Indeed, by this time, Gist's Marylanders were "the very flower" of General Washington's Army, including "men of honor, family, and fortune." Best represented by the elite Baltimore Independent Cadets, these well-trained Continentals of Smallwood's Maryland Battalion were not the kind of soldiers who would run at the first fire, like so many other American soldiers on this inglorious day. Smallwood's reliable men were the only Maryland troops in a division of Delaware, Pennsylvania, Connecticut, and New York soldiers.

During its baptismal fire, the Maryland Continental troops could rely fully upon the overall high quality of the equally tough Continentals from Delaware, who were mostly Irish. Perhaps the most smartly-uniformed troops in Washington's Army, the Delaware Celts proudly wore fancy blue uniforms trimmed in red. Symbolically, as if fighting for the liberty of the oppressed Ireland homeland so far away, the Irish Continentals from Delaware also wore tall leather and high-peaked hats, with the inspiring words, "Liberty and Independence" in large gilt letters.

Like Smallwood in fine-tuning the Maryland Battalion with endless drill and iron discipline, Colonel Haslet, born in Derry in northern Ireland and a former member of the Delaware State Assembly, had molded these Delaware soldiers, also of General Sullivan's Division, into crack troops by this time. But with Colonel Haslet on court martial duty with Smallwood, Major McDonough, another Celtic warrior, now served as a worthy replacement.

Like the Marylanders, the 750 Delaware soldiers were among the most disciplined Continental troops in Washington's Army. Additionally, these tough Maryland and Delaware Continentals were more formidable than most of Washington's troops today also because bayonets were fixed at the ends of their muskets. Despite the vast disparity in numbers, this added technical and psychological advantage

51

now made the Maryland and Delaware troops more of an equal match for the attacking British and Hessians, who prided themselves on the bayonet's use.

On this hot day of crisis on Long Island, the Delaware Continentals from the smallest colony were about to prove to be dependable comrades-in-arms to the Marylanders. Like so many of Washington's top officers, Colonel Haslet was fated to die in combat at the battle of Princeton, New Jersey, in early 1777. Thereafter, the colonel's fine infantry regiment would continue to fight the British and Hessians on one battlefield in the years ahead: the Scotch-Irish colonel's enduring legacy long after he had died on a New Jersey battlefield.

With fixed bayonets sparking in the late August sunshine, the soldiers of the Delaware battalion were first drawn up in a lengthy line on the side of a wooded elevation known as the Gowanus Heights, standing beside the Maryland troops. Side by side, the Maryland and Delaware soldiers had "stood upwards of four hours, with a firm and determined countenance, in close array, their colors flying, the enemy's artillery playing on them all the while, but not daring to advance or attack them though six times their number and nearly surrounding them," in Haslet's words.

These Maryland and Delaware Continental troops now found themselves in the vital tactical position during the largest battle–in regard to numbers engaged and the total number of casualties–of the American Revolution. Most significant, perhaps the revolution's fate now hung in the balance. Indeed, much now hinged upon the fighting capabilities of a relative handful of Maryland and Delaware soldiers, after the rout on the American left and center in what had become the greatest disaster of American arms to date. Both the end of the revolution and the fledgling American republic hardly before it had breath life were quite possible, if Stirling and his troops did not rise to the challenge.

Everything was now on the line, and the Marylanders and Delaware soldiers, who realized as much, stood at the very vortex of the storm. Nothing in the world seemingly could now stop the victorious British Army from reaping a decisive victory this day. General Howe, of Irish heritage like so many of the men who he faced on this summer day, was seemingly about to achieve the war's greatest success to end the rebellion once and for all, if only the sole remaining American troops on the field–Lord Stirling and the diminutive right wing–were swiftly overwhelmed.

While the 9,000 British left wing troops under General Grant continued to push north and toward the Gowanus Heights, only Lord Stirling's brigade now stood firm on the right flank, including the Maryland and Delaware Continentals. Also fighting with spirit before the western edge of Gowanus Heights was Ireland-born Colonel Hand and his roughhewn regiment of Pennsylvania riflemen, mostly Irish and Scotch-Irish, from the western frontier. In many ways, the last stand by the right wing of the collapsed American line was shaping up to the very much an Irish fight for survival and for the honor of old Ireland.

But, unable to withstand the mounting pressure, Colonel Hand and his hard-fighting Irish and other Pennsylvania militiamen of a battalion, under Colonel Atlee, fell back. Amid palls of smoke, they retired through the thin ranks of the Marylanders, whose line of blue stretched across the Gowanus Road remained intact, despite the steady pounding of British artillery.

Then, Lord Sterling ordered the entire line back to higher ground atop a hill on the western edge of the heights of Gowanus. Here, he consolidated his increasingly vulnerable position, while General Grant threw in additional British troops and applied more pressure from the south. Lord Stirling's defensive line was deployed in two ranks, which began to waver under the hammering of artillery fire and musketry. Nothing now remained of the American lines to the north and east, where the center and left had dissolved before the British onslaught. By this time, thousands of American defenders were either killed, wounded, prisoners, or run away on the war's greatest disaster to date.

This fiasco allowed the victorious British and Hessians from all across the field of strife to converge southward upon the last remaining Americans defenders in the field, Lord Stirling's troops on the right flank from the rear. After achieving success to the north and northeast in routing Sullivan's Division, Earl Cornwallis's troops descended south down the Gowanus Road to ease into the stabilized right and rear of the American right wing. In the way, the British now blocked the route of withdrawal, the Gowanus Road that led to Brooklyn Heights, for Lord Stirling and his hard-fighting soldiers to the north, or to the safety of the inner defensive line.

All the while, the fast-diminishing American right flank was threatened to be annihilated by increasing numbers of British and Hessian troops, which were hurled into the fray. These professionals in bright scarlet coats were some of the best trained fighting men in the world. Most important, if the British overwhelmed the American right wing, then thousands of withdrawing colonial troops would be surrounded and unable to escape across Gowanus Creek and Bay—the only open route with the Gowanus Road occupied by Cornwallis--to reach the safety of the inner network of American lines on Brooklyn Heights.

With battle-flags flying in the bright summer sunlight, Cornwallis troops continued to push south to the Old Stone House, built by Nicholas Van Vechte in 1699 at the intersection of the Gowanus Road with the Porte Road, just east of Gowanus Creek. The overwhelming numbers of the foremost redcoat attackers continued to swell with the arrival of additional British troops, who now closed in for the kill. It was only a matter of time before, General Grant, advancing north from the south along the Gowanus Road, and Lord Cornwallis, pushing south from the north by way of the Gowanus Road, easily crushed what little remained of the American right flank between them like a walnut. What little remained of Stirling's southern most wing was not only made more vulnerable from increasing losses, but also from the fact that many soldiers had run out of ammunition by this time.

Worst of all, a third of the entire British force, under Lord Cornwallis, now stood between Lord Stirling's troops and the Americans' inner defensive line. In stealthy fashion and before the Americans had realized it, Cornwallis' troops had gained the rear of the Maryland and Delaware troops, while a mass of Germans poured westward down the ridge from the east and toward the exposed flank. Lord Stirling's left flank was no more. His battle-line on the left and center was collapsed, after Atlee and many of his troops, with other of Stirling's men, had been surrounded, captured, and swept aside. By 11:00 a.m., only the Maryland and Delaware commands yet stood firm on the timbered ridge of Gowanus. No hope for survival now remained for Major Gist's Marylanders and Major McDonough's Delaware soldiers, or so it seemed.

With disaster staring him in the face and without orders or seemingly any hope for escape and with his ever-dwindling forces about to be encircled, Lord Stirling stood before his Maryland and Delaware troops, now facing north. He defiantly maintained his ground in the face of Cornwallis's advance down the Gowanus Road from the north. Meanwhile, Lord Stirling's remaining few troops continued to fight against General Grant's onslaught up the Gowanus Road from the south. All in all, three powerful British columns—Lord Cornwallis in the rear, or to the north;

General Grant in front, or to the south; and General Philip von Heister's Hessians on the left, or to the east–rapidly converged on Lord Stirling's force to crush it in a deadly vise grip from which there would be no escape. In typical Celtic fashion, Lord Stirling, the fiery Scotsman who felt that he had much to prove on this day, then made one of the boldest possible tactical decisions in such a no-win situation.

In the face of impossible odds and on the verge of disaster, a growing sense of desperation forced Lord Stirling to give the fateful order for Major Gist and his 400 Maryland Continental to attack northward up the Gowanus Road with the bayonet, while his remaining troops faced south to hold General Grant's advancing soldiers at bay as long as possible. Lord Stirling knew that the best defense was to take a bold offensive, if there was any chance to save those thousands of Americans attempting to escape northwest across Gowanus Creek. If any troops in General Washington's Army could slow the British onslaught of Lord Cornwallis, it was these well-trained and disciplined Marylanders.

With bayonets flashing in the late August sunlight, the Marylanders charged with a shout. Lord Stirling was no textbook soldier hampered by outdated rules, but a natural leader. Therefore, he not only ordered the Maryland troops to charge, but also led them forward along Major Gist. With Stirling and Gist leading the way, the Marylanders surged north down the slope of the western edge of the Gowanus Heights and toward the scarlet and blue-hued ranks poised around the Old Stone House. Here, Lord Cornwallis centered his position, bolstered by artillery, six-pounders, and hundreds of well-trained British troops, including Simon Fraser's Highlanders or the Seventy-First Regiment, and Hessian troops. While drummer boys beat their drums, Major Gist led his Marylanders onward with discipline to not only protect the American withdrawal but also with the intention of achieving tactical gains.

Around the Old Stone House, the veteran British and German troops could hardly believe their eyes: instead of giving up and surrendering as was expected and which was customary in Eighteenth Century warfare in such no-win circumstances, a small band of colonial soldiers from Maryland were now attacking with the bayonet, even while additional reinforcing British units poured down from the north and into this suddenly-strategic sector at the dusty crossroads of the Porte and Gowanus Roads to strengthen Lord Cornwallis's position.

Moving with firm step through a scorching fire as if they were on a Baltimore parade ground on a springtime morning, the attacking Maryland soldiers tore into the British with abandon. Here, they battled hand-to-hand with the redcoats, fighting against fate to reverse the tide. The Marylanders recoiled from the point-blank fire and flurry of jabbing bayonets, but were rallied by Major Gist. With battle flags waving in the sulphurous smoke that hung heavy in the humid air, they then charged again into the din with leveled bayonets. Despite devastating losses, the Maryland soldiers charged again and again, striking one blow after another. During the most vicious fighting of the day during the largest battle of the American Revolution, the Marylanders drove the hard-fighting British away twice from their defensive positions around the Old Stone House. But each time, Major Gist and his boys were eventually forced back by overwhelming numbers, who continued to converge upon them.

But by this time when so far advanced, the vulnerable Maryland Continentals were caught in a vicious crossfire of musketry, while artillery-fire tore gaps in their ranks. After having faced north to strike Lord Cornwallis's victorious legions, the Marylanders were now also punished by the fire of General Grant's forces attacking in their rear to the south.

In overall tactical terms, the Marylanders and their Delaware compatriots, who had advanced to the Marylanders' rear, were now practically surrounded by units of blue-uniformed Hessians, elite British grenadiers in scarlet, and the kilted soldiers from the Scotland's Highlands. Battling for Scotland's and their regiment's honor, these excellent fighting men were members of the Scottish 42nd Royal Highland Regiment, or the Black Watch Regiment. This famed regiment of Scottish Highlanders had fought with distinction at Fontenoy, Belgium, in 1745, where the Irish Brigade of the French Army won ever-lasting fame for a daring bayonet charge that won the day.

This disastrous tactical situation for the Maryland boys that all but ensured entrapment and annihilation forced the never-say-die Major Gist to become even more aggressive during the height of the day's crisis. Therefore, Gist once again ordered his soldiers to charge forward to break through the tightening scarlet and blue lines of crack troops. Incredibly, Lord Stirling, who was inspiring the troops, and Gist "launched a frontal assault on 10,000 British and Germans surrounding them," according to one estimation.

In total, Major Gist and his hard-fighting Marylanders charged numerous times, perhaps as high as half a dozen times, at the dense British and Hessian formations aligned around the vicinity of the stone Vechte House. Redcoats fired from the windows, taking advantage of their lofty perch to wreck more havoc. The intensity of the Marylanders' slashing attack to break out of the trap shocked Lord Cornwallis, who could hardly believe the fighting resolve of such a small band of Continentals. After all, the Maryland Continentals almost broke completely through the dense lines of red and blue, both British regulars and finely-drilled Hessians. In the process of thwarting the progress of the British and German onslaught, however, the attacking Marylanders were decimated until virtually nothing remained of the command.

In overall tactical terms, the Marylanders and Delaware troops were fighting a desperate rear-guard action in an attempt to save what little was left of the defeated American forces, buying time for thousands of Americans to yet escape across the Gowanus Creek and the surrounding wetlands to the safety of the inner defensive line of Brooklyn. Such a unfavorable tactical situation almost always called for a defensive stand against such odds. But this wisdom had been rejected by dynamic leadership team of Lord Stirling and Major Gist.

Instead of doing what was customary and expected by the British and Hessians, the Marylanders and Delaware Continentals had taken the offensive not once, but repeatedly. Most important, the successive charges up the Gowanus Road into the converging masses of Cornwallis's redcoats broke the momentum of the British onslaught, saving the day for the collapsed right wing of the American Army that faced destruction and the survivors of the routed left and center. Incredibly, the Marylanders even drove the British lines rearward at some points, briefly capturing two or three of British six-pounders positioned beside the Old Stone House. Gist's Continentals even captured a number of Hessian and British prisoners during the only American offensive success of the day. Only large numbers of arriving British troops had been enough to stop the sixth, and last, attack launched by Gist upon the embattled Vechte House sector, which was now strewn with a good many dead and wounded of both sides.

Most important for the future operations of Washington's Army, including at Trenton at year's end, the repeated hard-hitting attacks delivered by Major Gist's Maryland soldiers allowed large numbers of defeated Americans and the right wing's survivors to escape through the watery meadows, mill ponds, and salt marches of

Gowanus and across the deep waters of Gowanus Creek. Therefore, thousands of these troops were able to reach the last defensive line on the peninsula to live to fight another day in Washington's ranks.

Against the odds, the Marylanders' audacity and high sacrifice in life paid dividends that could hardly have been higher. Holding large numbers of General Clinton's and Lord Cornwallis's legions "in check by wonderful bravery until the rest of the Americans [of Lord Stirling' right wing] had crossed Gowanus Creek to safety [and] It was in this part of the action that one-third of the Marylanders were slaughtered, but they crowned themselves with glory and saved their brothers from annihilation." Indeed, the majority of American troops of the shattered right wing, even though their commander, Lord Stirling, was captured, escaped the disaster and certain capture to find safety within the American inner defensive lines. Even more, Stirling and Gist drew the enemy's attention away from the Brooklyn Line, where Washington and thousands of troops were vulnerable, stuck on the wrong side of the East River, isolated on Long Island, and separated from New York City. If the Brooklyn Line had been overwhelmed and Washington captured along with 9,000 men, then the revolution's end might well have resulted.

But the price of achieving tactical success on this day of disaster on Long Island was frightful. Of the 400 Maryland soldiers who marched into battle with fixed bayonets and a determination to turn the tide at any cost, a total of 256 were lost on the field. Either killed or wounded, the vast majority of these Maryland Continentals were now scattered across the open ground around the Old Stone, or Vechte, House and along the Gowanus Road. More than a 100 other Maryland men were captured or missing during the six desperate attacks against impossible odds. The high number of fatalities resulted not only from the repeated frontal assaults across the open ground before the Old Stone House, but also because the Hessians gave no-quarter as throughout the day, including crushing Sullivan's Division. The Germans in blue uniforms bayoneted some wounded Maryland soldiers lying helpless on the ground, slaughtering Gist's men because the British had falsely told them that the Americans had adopted a no-quarter policy toward the Hessians.

After the last attack on the Old Stone House sector, Major Gist ordered what few survivors remained to shift for themselves as best they could, hoping that as many men would escape as possible across Gowanus Creek to reach Brooklyn Heights. However, by this time, the vast majority of the young Baltimore major's troops lay dead or dying, missing, captured, or wounded.

Only Major Gist and seven other Maryland men escaped the slaughter, after racing through the salt marshes and swimming the deep, grayish-hued waters of Gowanus Creek and the mill ponds to escape to the safety of the inner defensive line on the peninsula. At least two Maryland soldiers, perhaps more, along with two Hessian prisoners, drowned in crossing deep Gowanus Creek, a tidal waterway, and the large mill ponds.

But despite the carnage and devastating losses, the Maryland soldiers brought back their bullet-tattered battalion colors, along with nearly thirty Hessian and British prisoners. Without exaggeration, one impressed American soldier described the performance of Smallwood's Maryland troops on this day: "Our men fought with more than Roman valor." And a British officer, with a rare sense of admiration for American troops, swore that the Maryland and Delaware Irish and Scotch-Irish "fought and fell like Romans" on bloody August 27.

But it was General Washington, watching the slaughter of Major Gist's Marylanders in the humid lowlands below from the high ground of the inner lines of the earthworks, who paid the finest tribute to the performance of the 400 Marylanders, mostly Irish and Scotch-Irish soldiers: "Good God! What brave fellows I must this day lose!" While almost all of the Maryland troops were either killed, wounded, missing, or captured. By comparison, only 31 of the 750 Delaware Continentals were killed.

For the Maryland troops who suffered around ten times as many casualties as the Delaware soldiers, they earned the widespread reputation throughout General Washington's Army as the "Tenth Legion." The fabled Tenth Legion was the legendary elite Roman legion of Julius Caesar, who personally raised this elite unit in Spain and made it his personal bodyguard, because of its superior fighting capabilities, discipline, and high esprit de corps. In fact, the Tenth Legion was the most famous legion of ancient Rome. The Tenth Legion's warriors served in Caesar's greatest victories, winning an unmatched reputation for hard fighting and reliability like the Maryland troops at Long Island.

One of Smallwood's men who been a casualty at Long Island was Captain Daniel Bowie. He was a member of the politically-powerful Bowie family of Upper Marlboro, Maryland, area in the Patuxent River and tobacco country of southern Maryland. The Bowie family had been forced to migrate first to northern Ireland, because they had been Jacobite rebels from the Scottish Highlands, and then to America. Captain Bowie would have a famous descendant who would be killed in another revolutionary struggle in the far-away northern province of the Republic of Mexico on March 6, 1836, James Bowie at the old Spanish mission known as the Alamo.

For the future, the overall morale and fighting spirit, when at its lowest ebb to date, was raised throughout Washington's Army by the stirring exploits of Major Gist and his Marylanders in the struggle around the Old Stone House. For their unmatched performance on this August day, Smallwood's Maryland Battalion became known throughout the army as the "Immortals" for their combat prowess. After all, they had not only survived a slaughter, but also saved not only the right wing of General Washington's Army on Long Island, but also other Americans of the center and left.

In addition, the Maryland Continentals under Major Gist had demonstrated for the first time that Continental troops could stand up to Europe's best troops. And these young Americans proved that they could repeatedly attack impossible odds and the finest professional troops in the world: a significant first milestone in the history of the fledgling United States Army. Performing like battle-hardened regulars and beating, for a time, some of the best professional soldiers of Europe, the Maryland troops had demonstrated at the battle of Long Island that these Continentals were the kind of soldiers, who would ensure that Washington's Army would become more formidable in the years ahead.

One unknown writer-historian summarized an undeniable truth: "The Declaration of Independence that was signed in ink in Philadelphia was signed in blood in south Brooklyn." What this anonymous author forgot to mention was that fact that much of this blood shed to ensure a new nation's independence at the battle of Long Island, or Brooklyn, was Irish and Scotch-Irish blood.

One of the few Maryland survivors was Major Gist. He could proudly claim one of the few outstanding tactical performances of an American commander on disastrous August 27. In time, Gist was destined to gain a general's rank, and he would also serve with distinction in the war in the South. After resettling to Charleston, South Carolina, after the war, Gist's took pride in a favorite son whose name indicated his father's revolutionary sentiments, States Rights Gist. As a general like his father in another struggle for self-determination, his son would be killed in the nightmarish attack on the Union fortifications at Franklin, Tennessee, on November 30, 1864.

Symbolically, the survivors of both Colonel Smallwood's First Maryland Battalion and Colonel Haslet's Delaware Battalion would be among the relatively few troops remaining in the thinned ranks of Washington's Army, which turned the tide of war at Trenton, New Jersey. All in all, the Maryland and Delaware Continental troops demonstrated at the battle of Long Island and afterward that they were the elite troops of the General Washington's Continental Army.

Chapter III: Reversing the Tide at Trenton, December 26, 1776

During the darkest days of the American Revolution by December 1776, large numbers of Irish and Scotch-Irish men were among the most steadfast soldiers in Washington's ever-thinning ranks. In disproportionate numbers, they refused to forsake the cause and desert like so many others, who had lost heart and faith in the revolution. In an example of typical Irish clannishness stemming from their distinctive Celtic-Gaelic culture and heritage, these soldiers from Ireland clung together to the bitter end. Consequently, they remained faithfully with their depleted regiments, that resembled skeleton organizations, after the disastrous loss of New York City.

By late 1776, the revolutionary struggle against Great Britain, and even the spirit of revolution itself, was gradually dying among the American people, who had lost hope for success. Prospects for success were bleak and never darker. Repeated American defeats and disasters for the amateur patriot soldiers at the hands of the British Army had all but broken the revolution's back. Consequently, throughout the thirteen colonies, morale plummeted to new depths.

Therefore, the number of enlistments in America's armies dropped dramatically, along with the ever-dwindling strength of General Washington's reeling army. Worst of all, General Washington's ragtag collection of undisciplined volunteers was yet primary an army in name only. This so-called "army" had yet to win a victory in a fast-failing resistance effort that was becoming little more than a comic opera to the hardened British professionals. Washington was becoming an object of widespread ridicule and derision on both sides. Quite simply, he was incapable of winning victory.

After disaster on Long Island, Continental Army had been driven out of New York City, the most strategic city in America, and beyond New York's borders. To gain breathing space and reorganize after losing New York City, General Washington's Army fled southwest across the marshy flat lands and hardwood forests of New Jersey, with the seemingly unbeatable British and German Hessians in close pursuit.

This fledgling army of colonial amateurs at war had already suffered four major defeats, and had retreated nearly a hundred miles southwest toward America's capital of Philadelphia. In only three months, General Washington and his Continental Army had lost large portions of three colonies. Nearly 90 percent of the Continental Army was simply no more. With each successive reversal, Washington's fledgling army had dissolved even more, disappearing like the ever-diminishing prospects for success. The high disease rates, battle losses, large numbers of prisoners-of-war, and massive desertions decimated General Washington's Army.

On the northern front, the ill-fated American effort to conquer Canada had ended in a fiasco. This humiliating setback ensured that Canada would never be a Fourteenth Colony, as so optimistically envisioned by the amateur politician-strategists of the Continental Congress. Knowing that the fate of hanging awaited them if captured, members of Congress fled from Philadelphia to escape the advancing British Army, reconvening in Baltimore.

Consequently, the onset of 1776's winter found the antagonists on either side of the broad waters of the Delaware River, with the Americans on the Pennsylvania side, to the west, and the British on the New Jersey side, to the east. At this time, General Washington's depleted army possessed almost no realistic chance for success against an opponent who seemed all but invincible by this time.

Never had the patriot cause reached a lower point than by the cold, gloomy days of December 1776: the conflict's darkest days. Thanks to a string of British victories and corresponding patriot disasters, popular support for the rebellion had been all but eliminated by early December 1776. Thousands of colonists had wavered in their commitment to what was clearly turning out to be a losing effort against the mighty British and their German mercenaries, signing loyalty oaths and forsaking the struggling for liberty.

For all practical purposes, the spirit of revolution had been practically extinguished from the hearts and minds from most Americans, who now either espoused neutrality or remained loyal to the Crown after changing sides. Throughout this bleak period, thousands of Americans simply refused to serve or deserted from Washington's Army in overwhelming numbers. Larger numbers of colonials were even enlisting in Loyalist units. The rebellion had seemingly all but collapsed by the approach of Christmas 1776. This was the belief of many of General Washington's soldiers, including Irishman Sergeant James McMichael of the Pennsylvania Rifle Regiment. With gloom, he wrote in an early December 1776 letter how "we are reduced to so small a number [that] we have little hopes of victory." But while Sergeant McMichael was pessimistic, he nevertheless remained faithfully in the thinned ranks like so many other Irish and Scotch-Irish soldiers of Washington's Army.

Indeed, at this crucial time when most colonists were either loyalist, neutral, or had deserted the patriot cause, one group of colonists remained in general more faithful and steadfast in the army's ranks in disproportionate numbers, the Irish and Scotch-Irish. Thanks to the lessons and searing memories of Irish history and their own and their ancestors' experiences in the Green Isle homeland, large numbers of the Irish and Scotch-Irish yet cling passionately to the faith of a new nation as firmly as Celtic-Gaelic culture itself. Consequently, unlike many non-Irish, or those of English descent, these soldiers from the Emerald Isle continued to fight year after year to ensure that America would never endure Ireland's tragic fate of subjugation.

Indeed, this significant development was partly due to the fact the Irish were long familiar with oppression and defeat at the hands of the British, which fueled their ancient blood feud and hatred of their conquerors. More than any other soldiers of Washington's Army, the Irish and Scotch-Irish knew well of the bitter legacies of Irish defeat and the British reprisals in the aftermath of each failed Irish rebellion. With seemingly no hope remaining for success, the relative handful of soldiers, including a disproportionate percentage of Irish and Scotch-Irish, remaining in General Washington's Army were among those very few, as wrote James Wilkinson, who made-up "the little band that faced the storm."

In general, the Irish and Scotch-Irish were the most determined soldiers in the ever-dwindling ranks of Washington's Army, especially at this time. Because of unique historical and cultural factors from the Green Isle and long experienced to adversity and oppression, these young men and boys in general were simply more resistant to the overall demoralizing affect of the recent defeats and disasters unlike so many others, especially the non-Irish, who deserted and gave up the struggle. For the Irish, this development occurred because this struggle against the British—who had been the enemy long before the first shots were fired at Lexington and Concord, Massachusetts—was in many ways more intimate, personal, and more deeply rooted in the Irish past. Even more than colonists of English descent because of their own personal experiences and those of their ancestors in Ireland, the Irish and Scotch Irish knew from personal experience that decisive British victory would be the first step in transforming America into another Ireland, where the defeated Irish people were persecuted and future generations were doomed to misery and poverty.

After all, the Irish of this revolutionary generation yet recalled the disaster for the Irish people resulting from the ill-fated Treaty of Limerick, which ended the Jacobite struggle to free Ireland of British rule. The treaty's signing had set the stage for the persecution and disenfranchisement of the Irish Catholic people for generations: a tragic fate and subjugation of a proud land and a distinctive Celtic-Gaelic people that was simply unimaginable to most Americans of English descent. In contrast to the colonists of English heritage, the Irish knew first-hand of British's wrath and vengeance not only on the battlefield, but also in subjugating a homeland. For centuries, the English invaders had viewed all Irish as little more than rebels deserving of only punishment, exile, or death.

Yet another reason caused so many Irish and Scotch-Irish patriots in general to remain steadfastly in General Washington's ranks at this critical hour more so than so many non-Irish soldiers, especially those of English descent. The American Revolution was a civil war among the Irish and Scotch-Irish, with many fighting as Loyalists or serving in large numbers in the British Army, after having been recruited in Ireland. Later in the war, the ruthless anti-partisan activities of Lord Francis Rawdon-Hastings' Corps, the Volunteers of Ireland, stirred a sense a vengeance among the Irish and Scotch-Irish patriots, especially in the South. As colonel, Lord Rawdon commanded this Irish corps that had been formed in Philadelphia, after the city's capture in September 1777.

Rawdon's highly-disciplined unit, at least on the battlefield, of Irish troops was inspired by a popular song dedicated to this Irish unit and sung on St. Patrick's Day, which included the following lyrics: "Success to the

Shamrock, and all those who wear it . . . Every foe surveys them with terror, But every petticoat wishes them nearer, So Yankee keep off, or you'll soon learn your error, For Paddy shall prostrate lay every foe . . . Let's see if like him [St. Patrick], we can't sweep off the vermin [,] Who dare 'gainst the sons of the shamrock stand [and] As long as the blessings of Ireland hang o'er us, The crest of Rebellion shall tremble before us, ..." Ironically, the first St. Patrick's Day celebrated in New York City was made festive by these hardy Irish soldiers in redcoats, when they occupied the city in March 1777.

Such threatening words by the Sons of Erin of the Volunteers of Ireland were not mere bravado, but strongly backed-up by the actions. Utterly ruthless in their commitment to crush the revolution by any means, these tough Irish troops often treated the American populace, men, women, and children, as enemies. In this sense, they acted almost like British and Anglo-Irish occupiers in waging war against the Irish people back in Ireland, destroying homes and crops and killing men and raping women. Demonstrating that a civil war also existed among the Irish of America like the general populace across the thirteen colonies, these Volunteers of Ireland were some of the most feared soldiers in the British Army by late 1776.

Atrocities committed by the Volunteers of Ireland even shocked the Hessians, who were well-known for giving no quarter to American soldiers after they had surrendered. This brutality had been fully demonstrated by the German Hessian troops during the battle of Long Island, New York, in August 1776. But in general, the Irish seemed to be even more merciless off the battlefield than the German mercenaries. For instance, one shocked Hessian lieutenant, Johann von Kraft, wrote how, "Lord Rawdon's Corps (Volunteers of Ireland) perpetrate the grossest robberies and even kill" local citizens of the New York area. Therefore, Washington's

70

Irish and Scotch-Irish had many old scores to settle, including to avenge not only the ruthless actions of the British and Anglo-Irish in Ireland but also those by the British Army, with such a high percentage of Irish in its ranks, in America.

Because of such strong motivations, "hundreds" of Irish and Scotch-Irish soldiers were destined to remain steadfast in Washington's ranks for the upcoming challenge of Trenton, playing a vital role in this key turning point of the American Revolution. Among the very few men who had answered his country's call in late December 1776 to join General Washington's fast-fading army was a sixty-two-year-old minister, John Rosbrugh. Carrying an old French musket from the French and Indian Wars, he had marched off to war from his Allen Township Presbyterian Church, where he had been the minister since 1769, in Northampton County, Pennsylvania, just northwest of Philadelphia, to lead a company of zealous Irish volunteers from the "Irish Settlement."

This "Irish Settlement," where distinctive Celtic-Gaelic culture and traditions yet thrived, consisted of migrants from primarily northern Ireland, or Ulster Province. The people of the "Irish Settlement" had passionately embraced the patriot cause from the beginning. The powerful Irish blend of religion and patriotism was seen in the fact that Minister Rosbrugh was chosen to command these Irish and Scotch-Irish soldiers. They had decided to reinforce General Washington and his depleted army, before it was too late when few other Americans were willing to come forth. Revealing that this was not only a community but also a familial response, the Celtic company from the "Irish Settlement" included the Parson Rosbrugh's four brothers, Francis, James, John, and Robert.

Even though General Washington could count relatively few troops in the Continental Army by early December 1776, nevertheless, these were the types of fighting men who the commander-in-chief could count upon during a crisis. In one of the war's most audacious decisions, General Washington decided to cross the Delaware River in the dead of night in an effort to capture the isolated Hessian garrison of Trenton, New Jersey. A string of small British outposts established by General William Howe, who had already decided to end campaigning for 1776's winter, in a too-lengthy defensive front along the New Jersey border and the Delaware River were vulnerable. Fortunately for Washington, these defensive positions and winter garrisons were isolated and beyond mutual-supporting distance of each other.

For his great gamble of attempting to cross the Delaware on a dark Christmas night for an early morning attack on Trenton on December 26, General Washington could rely upon only a relative handful of good men and dependable soldiers. Not surprisingly, a high percentage of these, both officers and men, were Irish and Scotch-Irish. One of the most reliable soldiers was Colonel Henry Knox, who was one of Washington's top lieutenants. He was the son of an Irish immigrant from Belfast. Knox now commanded Washington's artillery of eighteen guns with an expertise and skill second to none.

Another trusty officer who could be counted upon in the attack on Trenton was Irishman Colonel Edward Hand, age thirty-two. Before the war, Hand was a successful Lancaster, Pennsylvania, physician before the war. He was born at the town of Clyduff in King's County, Ireland, in late December 1744. Hand was educated in the study of medicine at Trinity College in Dublin. But quite unlike the vast majority of Irish migrants, Hand first journeyed to the New World, Philadelphia, in 1767 as the surgeon's mate of the Eighteenth Royal Irish Regiment, while wearing a redcoat and serving with considerable pride in the British Army. After duty on the western frontier and despite having been made an ensign in 1772, he resigned from British service two years later to settle in the Lancaster area. Here, west of Philadelphia and just east of the Susquehanna River, Hand made his home in this bountiful land known for its beauty and endless opportunities. Hand became an active member of St. James Church in Lancaster, and a respected community leader.

When the conflict erupted in 1775 and although recently married, Hand went to war with an enthusiasm that was typically Irish. He was elected as the lieutenant colonel of Colonel Thompson's Pennsylvania Rifle Battalion that later became the First Pennsylvania Regiment of the Pennsylvania Line. Hand was promoted to colonel and commanded the First Pennsylvania with skill by early 1776. Reflecting his Irish heritage and in honor of the Celtic-Gaelic land of his ancestors, Colonel Hand designed the regimental flag. This distinctive battle-flag was colored in a rich emerald green, representing the Irishman's native Emerald Isle homeland so far away.

Colonel Hand was destined to become one of the best officers in General Washington's Army, explaining his rapid rise in ranks, popularity, and esteem. Before the battle of Long Island, Washington had relied primarily upon Hand's intelligence to ascertain British strength and intentions after they landed on Long Island. For his upcoming performance at the battle of Trenton, Hand was destined to earn a general's rank in April 1777. He would then serve in the Upper New York campaign in 1779 against Great Britain's Indian allies, the mighty Iroquois, to ensure the safety of the western frontier settlements. Hand's brother, Matthew, served as a surgeon in General Richard Henry "Light Horse" Lee's Legion, which created in late November 1780.

Especially after the battle of Long Island, Washington also placed much faith in another Ireland-born officer of promise, Colonel John Haslet. He was born in Ireland like Colonel Hand. Haslet had studied to become a minister, but turned to medicine in Kent and Sussex Counties, Delaware, and then thrived in politics. As an astute politician and a natural leader, Haslet served as a member of the Delaware assembly before the war. Early military experience was gained by Haslet as a colonel of the local militia. As demonstrated in the battle of Long Island, the hard-fighting Delaware Continentals prove themselves to be some of most reliable troops in Washington's Army. Clearly, Haslet was an officer that the Virginia commander-in-chief could rely upon completely, especially during a crisis situation. Like so many of his young soldiers in the ranks, Colonel Haslet represented not only the colony of Delaware in Washington's Continental Army, but also the Green Isle so far away.

One of the faithful units now serving with Washington's diminutive army at this time was the First City Troop of Philadelphia. This elite cavalry command consisted mostly of Irishmen from the second largest city in the British Empire, after London on the Thames. Among these reliable troopers were the two Mease brothers, James and John, who had been born in Strabane, County Tyrone, Ireland. This fine Philadelphia Troops of Light Horse, led by Captain Samuel Morris, was destined to serve as General Washington's personal escort and guardians during the upcoming battle of Trenton.

With so much at stake—the revolution's life—Washington most of all needed highly-motivated, reliable soldiers, who were determined to win at any cost in part because they "hated British oppression." And no troops in all America possessed a greater hereditary "hatred" for the British than the Irish and Scotch-Irish, because of the searing Irish experience. By this time, this animosity—an undying source of patriotism among the Celtic-Gaelic warriors—was an undeniable reality that Washington fully appreciated. Therefore, the commander-in-chief was now determined to exploit this distinctive ethnic dynamic to the fullest.

Therefore, in part with this reality in mind, Washington

selected Colonel John Armstrong, who was born in Donegal, Ireland, for a special mission to Cumberland and Lancaster Counties, Pennsylvania, amid the fertile, picturesque Cumberland Valley, which was heavily-populated by Irish and Scotch-Irish. Colonel Armstrong's mission was to select as many Irish and Scotch-Irish soldiers as possible to reinforce what little remained of Washington's Army. Colonel Armstrong was a hero of the western Pennsylvania frontier. He had led the daring raid across the Allegheny Mountains to attack the Delaware village of Kittanning, located on the Allegheny River just north of the future site of Pittsburg, Pennsylvania, during the French and Indian Wars. The Irishman's surprise attack eliminated this principal source of Indian raids that had long ravished the western frontier. Armstrong's timely recruiting mission paid dividends, justifying Washington's decision to focus on recruiting the ever-combative Irish and Scotch-Irish, because so few other men, the non-Irish, would come forward to serve in the diminutive Continental Army at this time. Armstrong's son now served as a respected officer in the ranks of Washington's Army at Trenton.

At the time of Washington's crossing of the Delaware River, therefore, in the estimation of one historian, practically the "only men in the crossing that were not from [Lancaster County and] Cumberland County" and not Irish and Scotch-Irish were Colonel John Glover's hardy fishermen and sailors–who could claim ancestors from Cornwall--from the Atlantic port of Marblehead, Massachusetts, just north of Boston.

Indeed, Colonel Armstrong and his Irish and Scotch-Irish troops helped to set the stage for the Delaware River crossing and Washington's bold strike on the 1,500-man German garrison of Trenton. Ireland-born Colonel Samuel Griffin and 600 militiamen were dispatched to create a diversion in New Jersey to keep British troops from reinforcing the

Trenton garrison of well-trained Hessian soldiers.

An additional heavily Irish and Scotch-Irish effort was forthcoming to assist Washington's chances for mounting a successful surprise attack on Trenton. A member of the Friendly Sons of St. Patrick of Philadelphia, General John Cadwalader, led his division of New Englanders and Pennsylvania troops on another diversionary mission in New Jersey a dozen miles below Trenton. Among General Cadwalader's troops was Ireland-born John Barry, who was destined to win fame as the "Father of the United States Navy." With his warship under construction, the Irish captain from Philadelphia now voluntarily led a company of United States Marines at Trenton, while also serving as General Cadwalader's aide-de-camp. Born in Ballysampson, County Wexford in southeast Ireland where revolutionary sentiment against the British had often risen to the fore and migrating to America as a mate aboard an Irish sailing ship, Barry has provided a classic example not only of the legendary Irish fighting spirit, but also his dramatic rise from lowly cabin boy to wealthy Philadelphia ship-owner and master. In truth, Barry has deserved more recognition than the better-known John Paul Jones, who another Celtic naval commander, born in Scotland, for his naval exploits on the high seas.

Washington could also count on a dependable "hard-driving Scotch-Irish chieftain" in General James Ewing. He led many Irish and Scotch-Irish soldiers from the Cumberland and Susquehanna Valleys in southeastern and central Pennsylvania. These Irish and Scotch-Irish now served in the five regiments of General Ewing's Pennsylvania militia brigade. Hailing from the western frontier of Lancaster, Chester, Cumberland, and York Counties, Pennsylvania, these soldiers now hoped to save their homes and families on the Delaware's west side from future British invasion. But the majority of General Ewing's brigade consisted of two regiments from a single county, Cumberland which lay west of the Susquehanna, that was heavily settled by Irish and Scotch-Irish. General Ewing had descended from Irish parents who had migrated from northern Ireland to Pennsylvania in 1734.

On the coldness of the late evening of December 24, Christmas Eve, and just before the order to begin the march to cross the Delaware, Washington held a council of war with his top lieutenants. This meeting included two sons of Irish immigrants, General John Sullivan and Colonel Henry Knox, who assisted in the formulation of Washington's final plans for the multi-column crossing of the Delaware to attack Trenton.

With the enlistment terms of many soldiers about to expire at year's end which forced him to gamble upon an audacious offensive strike, Washington's watchword for the attack on Trenton was "Victory or Death." At this high level meeting, it was decided that three separate columns would cross the Delaware River at different points in the darkness, before descending upon the German garrison of Trenton to catch the Hessians by surprise with December 26's dawn. But this task would not be easy. Having yet to lose a single battle on American soil, this experienced Hessian brigade stationed at Trenton was commanded by Colonel Johann Rall. His German soldiers were highly-disciplined troops, who knew how to fight. Both Colonel Rall and his bluecoat Hessians had won laurels at the battle of White Plains in late October 1776 and especially in Fort Washington's capture in November 1776, the greatest disaster to befall American arms.

Washington's planned movement across the wide Delaware River was symbolic in many ways for the large percentage of Irish and Scotch-Irish in the ranks. For thousands of immigrants from the Emerald Isle, the Delaware River, linked to the Atlantic, had long served as the principal waterway entry for the Irish and Scotch-Irish to Philadelphia and the colony of Pennsylvania. Throughout the colonial period, the Delaware was the primary avenue by which the largest number of Irish and Scotch-Irish immigrants had flowed like a flood into the most heavily Irish and Scotch-Irish populated colony of the thirteen, Pennsylvania. Some Irishmen and Scotch-Irish in Washington's Continental Army had themselves first traveled to America's shores by way of the Delaware River only a short time before, or with their parents as youths. For instance, large numbers of Ulster migrants from northern Ireland had ascended the Delaware during the period of the 1730s-1750s. One such immigrant was Ireland-born Andrew Reed, who was now a successful merchant in Trenton, and the respected father of Washington's enterprising staff officer, Joseph Reed.

For the daring surprise attack upon Trenton with the revolution's existence now at stake, General Washington would march forward on a seemingly impossible mission, but with the assurance that he had a good many dependable Irish and Scotch-Irish were with him on this day of destiny to do or die. Indeed, at Trenton, around 40 percent of General Washington's main strike force of 2,400 soldiers were Irish and Scotch-Irish, while seven of his generals and four of his colonels were either born in Ireland or the sons of Irish parents.

While General Washington would lead the main column of the army in the attack, General John Sullivan, of Irish heritage like Colonel Knox, would led the strike force's other wing. In addition, Knox would be in charge not only of the army's artillery, but he also would direct Washington's main crossing of the Delaware. With a key assignment, Ireland-born Colonel Edward Hand and his Pennsylvania riflemen, of mostly Irish and Scotch-Irish descent, would block the Hessians' retreat from Trenton, after taking a defensive position on the Princeton Road to stop their flight, once the attack columns struck Trenton at first light, as planned.

And Thomas Read, a promising Irish officer who could proudly claim descendants from Dublin and whose brother, George Read had signed the Declaration of Independence in Philadelphia, commanded a battery of iron cannon. These small caliber guns had been transferred from a naval frigate–the George Washington-- that Read commanded and had been assigned to the Delaware River to protect Philadelphia from the ascent of British warships. Also in the attack column was Captain Read's brother, Colonel James Read.

A burning desire for revenge for so many past defeats and humiliations loomed large in the thinking of Washington's men at this time. Ireland-born Colonel Joseph Reed now acted as the capable adjutant general of the Continental Army, after having served as General Washington's aide. He was a young, promising attorney from Philadelphia, where so many Irish lived and worked. When British troops had mocked the American fighting capabilities with the bugle call of the fox-hunt at the battle of Harlem Heights, on Manhattan Island, on September 16, 1776, in anticipation that the colonial soldiers would once again run before the onslaught of British regulars, an incensed Colonel Reed, with his Irish temper rising, implored General Washington to strike back immediately in response to the taut. Washington, therefore, ordered his Continentals forward to drive the battle-hardened Scottish Highlanders of the famed Black Watch regiment from the field. Shocking these elite British troops, the attacking Americans succeeded in their mission. For the first time, Washington's soldiers forced elite British troops, the 42nd Highlanders no less, to turn and run on the battlefield: a significant psychological triumph for the inexperienced Americans.

Just recently Colonel Joseph Reed, the son of an Irish immigrant, had played a key role in imploring Washington that late December was in fact the perfect time to strike a blow on an over-confident enemy, and that Trenton was the best target. This tactical analysis was fitting, because Reed had been born in Trenton in 1741. He returned from receiving a fine education at a college in London to establish a successful legal practice in Trenton in 1765. On December 22, Colonel Reed, writing also in behalf of fellow Continental officers, had penned to Washington to prod him into offensive action: "Will it not be possible my dear Genl for your Troops or such Part of them as can act with Advantage to make a Diversion or something more at or about Trenton [as] our Cause is desperate & hopeless if we do not take the Oppy [opportunity] of the Collection of Troops at present to strike some Stroke."

That long-awaited "Stroke" would come on the early morning of December 26 at Trenton. Indeed, Colonel Rall's brigade was isolated and vulnerable, looming far from the nearest support troops stationed at Princeton and Bordentown, New Jersey. Besides providing sound advice to take the offensive, Colonel Reed was assigned by Washington to command part of a diversion of Pennsylvania troops south of Trenton to mask the main crossing nine miles north of Trenton at the Delaware River ferry of Samuel McConkey, who had been born in Ireland. Like most Irish, McConkey supported the patriot cause with a passion, providing Washington with yet another sound reason to cross at this point north of Trenton. Washington had long considered the young, capable Irishman named Reed to be not only one of his best officers but also one of his best friends.

Other reliable Irishmen served in Washington's depleted ranks, including Irish Private George Fullerton. He was a member of this mostly Irish cavalry unit known as the First City Troop of Philadelphia. Private Fullerton was one of the few Americans who was destined to be killed in the upcoming battle of Trenton. Another Ireland-born aide that General Washington trusted in full was Colonel Stephen Moylan of Cork, Ireland. Young and dashing, Moylan was a hard-fighting Irish Catholic from a wealthy Philadelphia merchant family with strong commercial and family ties back to Ireland. Moylan gained a fine education at a leading Catholic university in Paris, France. But, unfortunately, this Irishman was not present on the march to Trenton. Washington had given Moylan the key mission of hurrying General Charles Lee's and General Horatio Gates' forces south to join Washington's Army, before it was too late.

But the leading officer of Irish roots who would play the most important role in the offensive strike across the Delaware was Colonel Knox. By this time, the Ulsterman was one of Washington's most trusted and best lieutenants. Knox, the former Boston bookseller and the son of Belfast immigrants, was well-versed in military tactics and the lessons of history from his extensive readings. Most important, he was now the aggressive and innovative artillery commander of Washington's Army: invaluable qualities for the upcoming fight.

A decision that would paid dividends at Trenton, Colonel Knox had recently convinced Washington to increase the size of his artillery arm for the attack. Convinced that artillery was the key to victory in warfare, Knox was proficient at skillfully utilizing the firepower of the artillery arm to the maximum affect. Knox also knew how to masterfully integrate artillery with infantry in the most effective manner to maximize their combined strength, while ensuring that they would act in close unison on the battlefield. And this capable son of Irish immigrant parents was about to demonstrate as much at Trenton. Colonel Knox's opinion that artillery was the key to victory was destined to be proved valid at Trenton.

Consequently, Washington's strike force now possessed a

large number of artillery pieces out-of-proportion to the number of infantrymen. With his eighteen artillery pieces accompanying the main column under Washington, Knox planned to overwhelm Colonel Rall's garrison with artillery firepower. Besides the inclement weather, much of the delay in crossing the Delaware would result in getting so many guns across the river in the cold darkness. But the decision to bring such a large number of cannon across the river would shortly pay dividends, as General Knox had envisioned with tactical clarity.

Under dark skies leaden with moisture, General Washington's troops mustered for the usual late afternoon parade on a snowy Christmas Day. Unknown to the common soldiers in the ranks, this afternoon muster was in fact the assembly time and point for the beginning of the march to the Delaware River. As quietly as possible, General Washington led his silent troops to the muddy banks of the Delaware River. He then ordered his soldiers to cross over the dark, ice-choked river in large wooded Durham boats during the frigid Christmas night. One who fell into the Delaware's freezing waters in the blackness was Colonel Haslet. Nevertheless, his Irish spunk and fighting spirit kept him in the ranks, doing his duty on a freezing night. In fact, the Ireland-born colonel would march "ten miles on severely swollen legs and fought a battle without compliant."

Knox skillfully orchestrated getting both the army and its artillery across the river on the frigid night. Washington planned to attack Trenton with three divergent, widely-separated columns that were to converge on Trenton. However, this was an overly-complex tactical plan, ensuring problems along the way. Such an ambitious tactical undertaking of crossing a river on a winter night, coordinating multiple strike columns, and attacking at a precise moments has often resulted in disaster in the annals of military history.

While Washington and his Continental regiments of around 2,400 soldiers crossed the Delaware at McConkey's Ferry nine miles above Trenton to attack the town from the north in the main attack, General Ewing's 1,000 militia, mostly Irish and Scotch-Irish soldiers, from the Cumberland Valley crossed the river at Trenton's Ferry just below Trenton to take a defense position on the south bank of Assumpink Creek, which ran along the town's southern border to enter the Delaware just south of town. Ewing's assignment was to block the German's escape route while Washington struck Trenton from the north.

But by the time the Americans had crossed the wind-swept, ice-clogged Delaware, the delicate timetable for striking Trenton at dawn on December 26, as General Washington had so optimistically planned, was in shambles. Indeed, the overly-ambitious plan for a multi-column crossing and rapid decent upon Trenton had fallen apart by this time. Both General Cadwalader column, south of Trenton that was to attack Bordentown to prevent the reinforcement of Trenton, and General Ewing's column, also below Trenton, which were to have crossed the river near Trenton, were thwarted. Nether column could achieve their tactical objectives.

Unable to cross the river because of the heavy ice flows and stormy weather, Ewing's effort was aborted. While General Ewing failed to get into a position to block the Hessian retreat southward from Washington's upcoming main attack to the north, General Cadwalader could not strike Bordentown, because he could not get his artillery over the Delaware. Cadwalader's diversion likewise floundered with comparable dismal results to match Ewing's failure. While Ewing's columns remained on the Pennsylvania side of the Delaware River at the decisive moment when Washington attacked Trenton, Cadwalader's men crossed the river, but would arrive too late to play a role in Trenton's capture.

Therefore, two of the three attack columns were out of operation at the most critical moment. Ironically, these multiple failures considerably simplified Washington's too-complex, intricate battle-plan to actually enhance overall chances for success. Seemingly frustrating Washington's plan to surprise the Hessians at sunrise, the failure of two of the three assault columns might have deterred Washington's decision to attack had he been aware of these developments.

Consequently, only General Washington's main column of Continental troops converged upon Trenton from the north--and another column under General Sullivan who advanced south down the river road to strike Trenton from the west after Washington had divided his own force upon crossing the river--well after sunrise to gain a suitable position to deliver the belated attack. By this time, however, General Washington's overall tactical plan to attack at dawn was now several hours late. Nevertheless, once unleashed, the timing of the American attack was superb. Two attack columns, which had advanced south and parallel along two adjacent road leading south to Trenton from Johnson's and McConkey's Ferries, struck simultaneously. Despite the missed dawn timetable and now at 8:00 a.m., the timing of the unleashing of the two attack columns surging through the swirling snow flurries and pelting sleet caught the Germans completely by surprise.

After marching along the river road in the cold darkness, the right wing of the army under General Sullivan, the First Division, emerged from the dark forests to hit Trenton from the west, while the left wing under General Nathaniel Greene, the Second Division farther east, struck Trenton from the northwest. American troops, including those under Ireland-born Colonel Hand who commanded mostly Irish and Scotch-Irish soldiers from Pennsylvania, had already blocked the Princeton Road as ordered. Both wings simultaneously struck Trenton and its hapless German garrison.

With typical Irish aggressiveness for which he was well-known, General Sullivan led his attackers of the right wing forward to overwhelm Hessian resistance, while the left wing under General Greene, led by General Washington in person, struck hard in three separate assault columns. At the head of his New Hampshire troops who he had drilled relentlessly with the bayonet, Colonel John Stark, a Scotch-Irish frontier leaders and former officer of Major Robert Roger's Rangers of the French and Indian War fame, and his men pushed forward and presented a row of bayonets: a sight alone that astounded the Germans. On this cold morning and like so many Irishmen in the ranks, the hard-fighting Colonel Stark, who already won fame for heroics at Bunker Hill, was determined to "live free or die."

The attacking Americans of both divisions swept all before them. Irishman Sergeant James McMichael, of the Pennsylvania Rifle Regiment, wrote with pride how: "We drove them furiously." Hessian resistance crumbled before the American onslaught. An Irishman from Virginia, Sergeant Samuel McCarty described in simple terms how the stealthy Americans "Came there about daybreak and beat the dam[ned] Hessians."

As Colonel Knox had planned and especially with many American flintlock muskets in non-firing condition from the wet, cold weather, the large number of artillery pieces were quickly deployed to play a leading role in decimating Hessian resistance. Blasts from Knox's cannon broke up the German attempts to rally. With the dampness having diminished the firing capabilities of the attackers' muskets, Knox's artillery rose to the fore, sweeping the principal streets of Trenton, where the Hessians hoped to form. These booming guns of the son of Irish immigrants were especially effective, playing a vital role in reaping the ultimate victory at Trenton. As he had anticipated, Knox's reliance on artillery firepower turned the tide of battle, sealing the fate of the doomed Hessian brigade.

But it was not just Colonel Knox's artillery that rose to the challenge on this snowy morning in the little town of Trenton. When Colonel Rall rallied some Hessian soldiers and then attempted to launch a counterattack with the bayonet to strike Washington's flank and restore the Germans' sagging fortunes, Ireland-born Colonel Hand led his Pennsylvania riflemen, mostly Irish and Scotch-Irish, forward with war-cries of the western frontier. As if fighting Native Americans for possession of the homeland as in the past, the Pennsylvanians then quickly maneuvered into good firing positions from where they blasted away to inflict more damage into the Hessian ranks. The combined affect of musketry and Colonel Knox's artillery thwarted the last German attempt to reverse the battle's course.

With a large percentage of Hessian officers cut down, including the mortally wounded Rall, and with a good many German soldiers dead or wounded, surrender became the only alternative for the hard-hit Hessians. In one of the war's boldest strikes, General Washington had captured Trenton and eliminated the German garrison with one masterful stroke. The American surprise attack netted nearly a 1,000 Hessian soldiers and six cannon. A full brigade of well-trained, splendidly-equipped German troops, some of the finest soldiers in the British Army, were swiftly eliminated by Washington's unexpected strike that shocked London and British commanders on both sides of the Atlantic. Neither British government or military leaders could hardly fathom how a ragged, ill-trained force of colonial soldiers commanded by a "general" who never won a battle could have possibly won a dramatic victory, after they seemingly had been all but vanquished by late December 1776.

Consequently, the surprising victory at Trenton was a moral and psychological success that played a key role in turning the American Revolution's tide. Washington's unexpected victory, exactly when the fortunes of the often-defeated Continental Army and the infant nation were at an all-time low point, lifted morale for the patriot cause throughout the colonies. The seemingly unbeatable momentum of a long string of British victories had been shattered on the snowy banks of the Delaware, where General Washington achieved a much-needed inspirational victory over the formidable Hessians, who were considered invincible.

In waging war against the world's strongest power, a religious people, both Protestant and Catholic, across the thirteen colonies viewed the unexpected victory at Trenton as God's confirmation of the righteousness of the patriot cause, after so many recent disasters. Americans across the land now began to see that the best enemy troops of the world's great superpower were not at all invincible: a key realization and understanding that helped to fuel the resistance of a people's war, a guerrilla conflict, and the eventual winning of a lengthy war of attrition.

Perhaps a British officer, Captain John Bowater, best explained the importance of the improbable victory at Trenton, Washington's most brilliant stroke of the war, in a most revealing letter: "The Business was done if it had not been for this affair . . . ." Clearly, General Washington's success at Trenton was a major turning point of the American Revolution. Most significant, this was a dramatic victory won largely by a disproportionate number of Irish and Scotch-Irish soldiers, both officers and enlisted men, who had refused to forsake the dream of an independent nation during the revolution's darkest hour like so many others.

Chapter IV: Great Gathering of the Celtic-Gaelic Clans, Victory at Kings Mountain on October 7, 1780.

While the Trenton story has been become one of the most famous of the American Revolution, some of the most important patriot victories in the South, which were as equally significant as turning points of the revolutionary war, have been relatively overlooked by historians. One such engagement of considerable important strategic consequences was fought amid the dense hardwood forests of Kings Mountain, South Carolina. The overemphasis of American historians in concentrating primarily on Washington's campaigns in the north and middle colonies has led to the minimizing of the importance of key battles in the South, especially Kings Mountain.

Prospects for a successful American resistant effort in the South never looked more bleak than by the early autumn of 1780, after Charleston's capture in the late spring of 1780 by the forces of Sir Henry Clinton. Not long thereafter, the British conquest of the South, orchestrated by the capable Lord Cornwallis who took over for Sir Clinton, had been seemingly achieved. British forces had not only conquered the South's most vital and strategic colony, South Carolina, but also Georgia. Resistance had all but collapsed, except for isolated guerrilla bands that only found refuge in the deepest cypress swamps of the South Carolina lowlands.

Here, in the South, most Americans were either neutral or Loyalists. Large numbers of colonists reaffirmed their allegiances to the Crown with the American resistance crumbling across the South, especially after the disastrous defeat of General Horatio Gates's Continental Army at Camden, South Carolina, August 16, 1780. On this infamous day, the American militia was routed and fled in panic, leaving the tough Maryland and Delaware Continentals, including veterans of the battle of Long Island, on their own to be crushed by British and Loyalist forces, including the red uniformed "Volunteers of Ireland." They were eventually overwhelmed by British forces in a clash that revealed the horrors of civil war among the Irish, and the fleeing Americans were pursued by Tarleton's cavalrymen. In efficient, business-like fashion, the last American army in the South had been easily vanquished by Lord Cornwallis. A British no quarter policy destroyed morale and additional lingering support for the cause of independence.

Perhaps all that now stood between the complete British conquest of the South and any American chance of eventually winning the war in this theater were the lingering vivid memories of English oppression in Ireland in the hearts and minds of the Irish and Scotch-Irish people of the Piedmont and the western frontier regions, including the untamed land on the west side of the Blue Ridge, or the Appalachians. Here, west of the Proclamation Line of 1763 and after the Cherokee's defeat in 1761, the Irish and Scotch-Irish had settled along the broad, rich valleys drained by the southwest-flowing Holston, Clinch, Nolichucky, and Watauga Rivers that flowed toward the mighty Tennessee River of the Mississippi River Basin. Not unlike departing Ireland for America's shores, they had left North Carolina and Virginia in search of new and more fertile lands to the west. Mostly Scotch-Irish, these settlers became known as the "over mountain men," and their new land west of the mountains would eventually become the state of Tennessee.

After the Camden disaster, among those few patriots yet resisting in the South were isolated guerrilla bands dominated by diehard Irish and Scotch-Irish. For instance, among those few resisting in the South included partisan leader Captain John McClure, who, with his sons, fought with the guerrilla band led by Thomas Sumter. Known as the "Carolina Gamecock" for his feisty fighting style, Sumter, a defiant Celtic leader who was the son of a Welch redemptioner, waged war against the British in the swamps and humid lowlands of South Carolina. Another Scotch-Irish guerrilla commander in South Carolina was Captain Thomas Brandon of Fairforest, South Carolina.

But the minor successes won by small patriot detachments were not sufficient to bring decisive victory or deny the British domination of the conquered South. Only a large number of Americans of a professional army could achieve that kind of victory. After General Gates's Army was vanquished at Camden, however, no American Army existed in the entire South. Basking in the glow of victory, Lord Cornwallis, therefore, laid plans to advance north into the Upper South to complete the South's conquest.

In many ways, the real story of the battle of Kings Mountain and the decisive patriot success achieved in October 1780 resulted from a spontaneous, traditional uniting of hundreds of western frontiersmen of Irish and Scotch-Irish descent. This development was not unlike the uniting of the traditional Celtic-Gaelic clans of Ireland or Scotland in battling against the English interlopers, who sought to possess the Irish ancestral homeland and impose their culture and religion upon the native inhabitants. Because of this Americanized uprising of the remote mountain Celtic-Gaelic clans, the battle of Kings Mountain was destined to become the greatest militia victory of the American Revolution, and a major turning point of the war in the South.

These mostly Irish and Scotch-Irish patriots of the Kings Mountain army were the so-called "overmountain" men, who had settled west of the Appalachian Mountains. The emergence of an unknown ghost army of frontiersmen, suddenly rising out of the dark depths of a primeval wilderness and not previously known to exist by either American or British commanders, was to become the only obstacle that could possibly thwart the grand fulfillment of Lord Cornwallis' ambitious strategic plan of the South's conquest.

Lord Cornwallis was the most vigorous British commander in America by this time. Cornwallis' strategic plan for conquering the South was based upon his army pushing north through the red clay hills and pine forests into North Carolina from his Charleston base. Then, Lord Cornwallis planned to link with another British Army in Virginia to smash all colonial resistance, which was already fast-fading away across the South. Then, the South's conquest would be complete, leading to the division of the colonies, with only the middle and northern colonies remaining unconquered. British forces could then concentrate on the conquest of the north, and then systematically end the rebellion against the Crown.

Indeed, the British campaign in the Deep South was crucial for the overall strategic plan for winning the war, because the British had already overwhelmed South Carolina, Georgia, and held the vital city of New York. And by early 1780, nothing seemed to stand in way to stop this ambitious British strategic plan to divide and conquer. However, like the rising of the ancient Celtic-Gaelic clans of Ireland and Scotland against the English invaders during centuries of Irish history, the Irish and Scotch Irish settlements along the Piedmont of Virginia and North Carolina and the untamed region on the other, or west, side of the Blue Ridge, now Tennessee, suddenly came alive. This general rising among the frontier people was destined to provide an unexpected source of resistance, when most needed and least expected by colonial leaders, the Continental Congress, and especially the British. These remote western settlements on both sides of the Blue Ridge were destined to provide the vital manpower and resources for a frontier uprising that would turn the war's tide in the South.

The frontiersmen who rose up as one from their mountains sanctuaries were largely Irish and Scotch-Irish.

These Celtic-Gaelic settlers were determined that their remote settlements and this new fledgling nation would not be conquered by the British like their native homeland of Ireland. By this time, the Irish and Scotch-Irish frontiersmen were known far and wide as the Long Hunters, or the Long Knives. Acclimating thoroughly to their wilderness environment, they had often defeated the Native Americans, especially the Cherokee, on their own terms by fighting Indian style. Their most recent success came during Lord Dunmore's War at the October 1774 battle of Point Pleasant. Here, these mostly Scotch-Irish frontiersmen from the Holston and Watauga River Valleys west of the Appalachians rose to the fore under their Scotch-Irish commander, General Lewis.

While simultaneously battling the native inhabitants, these feisty Irish and Scotch-Irish also had repeatedly defied colonial authorities and the Crown. Therefore, for these frontier Irish, resistance was very much a way-of-life, almost an unthinking, reflexive response. From an untamed and uncharted wilderness region unknown to leading colonial officials on the east coast, these backwoods Celts were also known as the Backwater men of the remote Watauga River country on the west side of the imposing Blue Ridge.

As could be expected from the elitist viewpoints of the British aristocracy, these western frontiersmen were held in utter contempt, especially among higher ranking military and government leaders who viewed them as barbarians: a fatal underestimation of an opponent. In the contemptuous words of General Thomas Gage, who saw the western frontiersmen as little more than "white savages [who] live like Indians"--ironically, the same kind of low regard that the British had long held of the native Irish of the Emerald Isle. But the common soldiers among the lower ranks of the British and Loyalists knew these hardy westerners from their mountainous wilderness simply as the "Yelling Devils" from hell, and for ample good reason.

Most of all, these hardened Scotch-Irish frontiersmen knew how to fight. They possessed the capabilities to thoroughly vanquish an opponent. Many of the newest settlers to this remote frontier region were North Carolina militiamen, who had defeated the Cherokees in 1776. At that time, they had caught their first glimpses of the fertile lands west of the Appalachians, after the militia had gathered from four states–North Carolina, Virginia, Georgia, and South Carolina--with the approval of the Continental Congress to eliminate the Cherokee threat. Victory in the Cherokee War had brought a new flood of settlers from both North Carolina and Virginia to the frontier settlements west of the mountains.

New settlers, including recent Irish immigrants, now mixed with the old time residents of the westernmost tier of settlement beyond the Appalachians. Among the founders of the Watauga community was William Bean. Born in 1716 and a savvy Indian trader, Bean had been the first Scotch-Irish settler of record (1769) in the fertile lands of the Watauga Valley. He was destined to serve as a respected captain at Kings Mountain, battling for the land he loved.

When word first arrived that a strong British force under the Scottish chieftain Major Patrick Ferguson, who had gained experience in smashing a French revolt on St. Vincent and won fame in the 1777 campaign against Washington's Army, was about to launch an invasion of North Carolina, these Irish and Scotch-Irish came together almost instinctively like their Irish forefathers against the English invaders of their homeland so long ago.

Born in Scotland in 1744, London-educated, and the privileged son from a high-ranking family, Ferguson was every inch a fighter. Most of all, he knew how to put down rebellions, getting his hands both dirty and bloody. Besides knowing how to keep white colonials in their place, Ferguson had also early gained recognition for ruthlessly crushing a slave revolt in the Caribbean island of Tobago, gaining valuable experience in art of counter-insurgency in the tropics.

Consequently, the homespun frontier westerners had become especially alarmed when they received a direct threat from Major Ferguson that "if they did not desist from their opposition to British arms, he would march his army over the mountains, hang their leaders, and lay their country waste with fire and sword." To exploit the overwhelming Camden success, Ferguson was now determined to "finish this business," as he wrote to General Cornwallis on October 5, and win glory for himself and his men.

Clearly, like others before him, including the Indians, Major Ferguson had seriously underestimated his homespun opponents in buckskin and hunting coats. If he had planned to scare the western frontiersmen into signing loyalty oaths to the Crown by way of such threats which had worked so well in New Jersey in 1776-1777 or in the Caribbean, then he was now badly mistaken. Ferguson's brash psychological warfare back-fired immediately. However, Ferguson was only blustering. At only age thirty-six and with two decades of sold service, he was yet a gentleman officer, who detested the ruthless actions of "Bloody Tarleton." Instead of cowing the western frontiersmen as planned, he had only incensed them to pick up their long rifles and go to war.

Clearly, Ferguson's words were taken as no idle threat in part because the major's troops had already plundered and burned rebel houses and farms in the South. Therefore, the western frontiersmen took Ferguson's threats as seriously as if they had received reports that Native Americans were planning to attack the western settlements. Major Ferguson and his American Loyalists had been thorough in their attempts to stamp out rebellion in the South. Especially rising the ire of the Irish and Scotch-Irish was the fact that the Loyalists not only often waged no quarter warfare, but also burned churches, both Catholic and Presbyterian. Ferguson quite correctly ascertained that these houses of worship were the dens of revolutionaries, where men and women were inspired by the words of fiery patriotic ministers.

Other than Tarleton, Major Ferguson was the most effective lieutenant of Lord Cornwallis but without Tarleton's mercilessness. The burning of Presbyterian churches of the Scotch-Irish inflamed the Presbyterian reverends, who also took up flintlocks. Having learned from history's lessons, they and their parishioners feared a repeat of the suppression of their religion as in Ireland. Consequently, all across the western frontier, Presbyterian reverends, mostly of Irish descent, implored the Celtic-Gaelic people of the western frontier to rise up as one and "to resist in something akin to holy war."

Indeed, the western frontiersmen answered the call of both their respected religious and community leaders, after Isaac Shelby, a fiery Celtic-Gaelic leader and a longtime vanquisher of Native American threats, and John Sevier, a natural leader and Indian fighter who had migrated from western Virginia to the Watauga settlement in 1775 and then moved on to the Nolichucky settlement in 1778, decided to eliminate Ferguson. Sevier was the principal leader of the Watauga settlements by this time. Most important, these two battle-hardened, frontier colonels swore that the Scotland-born Ferguson would never cross the mountains to wreak havoc on the western settlements nestled along the Clinch, Holston, Nolichucky, and Watauga Rivers.

As years of Indian warfare had demonstrated to one and all, the best way to accomplish this feat was to surprise the enemy by striking first. In a spontaneous Celtic-Gaelic rising to launch an expedition to defend their homeland by way of a preemptive strike, the frontiersmen mustered by the hundreds in the broad valley of the Watauga River at Sycamore Flats, or more commonly known as Sycamore Shoals, near the end of September 1780.

The flats lands of Sycamore Shoals had long served as a natural gather place for the frontiersmen. Social events, picnics, games, barbecues, and horse races had been held on these grounds for some time. Here, at Sycamore Shoals located just of the west side of what is today known as the Smoky Mountains of northeast Tennessee, not far from the confluence of the Holston and Watauga Rivers, the mountain men "on the[se] Western waters" west of the Appalachians gathered to defend their homeland and frontier system of free government of their own making that guaranteed "pioneer equality"–the Watauga Association--in the cooling early fall weather of late September 1780. Indeed, the Watauga Association had established a free governing community–America's first–before the signing of the Declaration of Independence.

Emerging from the misty forests covering remote mountaintops and the yet unmapped deep valleys of the Watauga, Clinch, Holston, and Nolichucky Rivers, these Celtic-Gaelic warriors prepared to embark upon an offensive campaign. As conceived by Colonels Shelby and Sevier, this expedition over the mountains would be a preemptive strike to destroy the advancing forces of Major Ferguson, before he struck first. Such a strategy was a western frontier requirement in wartime in order to keep an invader as far away from the homeland and families as possible: a brutal lesson of survival on the frontier learned by these westerners from battling Native Americans for decades. After all, many of these same frontiersmen had gathered an identical manner in early September 1774 to defeat the Shawnee, Delaware, and their allies in an all-day battle of Point Pleasant, Virginia, now West Virginia.

The popular Celtic-Gaelic commander who was destined

to lead the men of Kings Mountain was Colonel William Campbell of Washington County, Virginia. He commanded the unruly, tough Virginia riflemen from the cloud-wreathed mountains of the Old Dominion. From Highland ancestors of Scotland who had migrated to northern Ireland to become a new breed of people known as the Scotch-Irish by the Eighteenth Century, Campbell was handsome, with red hair and blue eyes, revealing his Celtic-Gaelic heritage. Campbell was a hard-nosed frontier fighter, who fought Indian-style with a skill that equaled those of the Native Americans.

Like so many other Irish and Scotch-Irish, the Campbell family had migrated from northern Ireland to the appropriately named Scotch-Irish town at the foothills of the Alleghenies, Donegal, Lancaster County, Pennsylvania in 1726. Then, they moved south to the fertile Great Valley of Virginia around 1730, searching for better lands and new opportunities. Here, in Augusta County, Virginia, this transplanted Protestant Irish family had prospered, before moving farther west to the remote valley of the Holston River on the mountain's west side. Colonel Campbell was the inspirational Celtic-Gaelic clan leader of "the Scotch-Irish patriots of the Holston Valley" and several hundred Virginians.

At Kings Mountain, Colonel Campbell's top lieutenant was the son of Irish immigrants, Major William Edmondson. He was a veteran of the victory against the Indians at Point Pleasant in 1774. Eight members of the Celtic-Gaelic Edmondson clan were destined to fight at Kings Mountain. All of the Edmondson boys served as officers, with four destined to become casualties during the close-range fighting at Kings Mountain. Lieutenant William Edmondson and Captain Robert Edmondson were fated to be killed in the upcoming battle.

But the most renowned Celtic-Gaelic leaders from the

lands west of the Blue Ridge was Colonel Shelby, who was a legendary Indian fighter. He was the kind of popular frontier commander who would immeasurably enhance the chances for success against Major Ferguson and his American Loyalists in redcoats during the showdown at Kings Mountain. His brother, Major Evan Shelby, Jr., was Isaac's top lieutenant at Kings Mountain, and brother Moses Shelby led a company of frontiersmen. Natural leaders of the western frontier, these men were savvy Indian fighters, who also knew the ways of the forest as well as the Native American people. In 1779 during a preemptive strike, Evan Shelby and John Sevier, destroyed nearly a dozen hostile Indian towns of the Chickamauga faction, on Chickamauga Creek near Lookout Mountain, Tennessee, and the Upper Creeks, now allied with the British who had supplied them with arms.

Irish and Scotch-Irish chieftains from both sides of the Blue Ridge included men like the McDowell brothers of North Carolina, including Major Joseph McDowell, who was destined to lead Burke County, North Carolina, troops on both sides of the Appalachians in the struggle for possession of the Piedmont and then at Kings Mountain. Commanding North Carolina militiamen as an elusive partisan chieftain, Charles McDowell knew that he would need the assistance of the "over mountain men" to help to turn the tide in the South. The McDowell boys were the sons of Irish immigrants, who had braved the arduous Atlantic passage of around two months, if winds were favorable, before settling in Pennsylvania. The McDowell family then migrated to the Shenandoah Valley, finding a home around Winchester, Virginia.

But it would take more than a traditional hatred of the British and a traditional gathering in the mountains of the Celtic-Gaelic clans to defeat this emerging threat in the form of Major Ferguson and his well-trained Loyalist soldiers. For the lengthy push over the Blue Ridge and into the lands east of the mountains, considerable resources were first needed for the successful conducting of the campaign. A good many provisions were required for the long ride on horseback by the expeditionary force southeastward into the Piedmont of North Carolina and South Carolina. Supplies, bullets, and ammunition were necessary to bestow greater capabilities upon these individualist frontiersmen to meet the upcoming challenge. In order to launch this ambitious expedition, these supplies had to be purchased, but cash on the western frontier, especially west of the mountains, was scarce.

But fortunately in the hour of greatest need, a frontier Irishman rose to the fore. One of the chief financiers of this frontier expedition was a native of Antrim County, Ireland, John Adair. He had migrated from Ireland in 1772 to settle in the wilderness of the Holston River Country. His son, John Adair, Jr., picked up a rifle to join the gathering frontiersmen at Sycamore Shoals for the expedition over the mountains to repel the invader, before the hated Loyalists reached the west side of the mountains, as feared. Adair was the chief state official who relegated the sale of North Carolina lands, and he was in charge of the Sullivan County land office, and despite no authority or instructions to direct any money for the expedition, because, in Adair's words, "it belongs to the impoverished treasury of North Carolina . . . but, if the country is over-run by the British, our liberty is gone." The Irishman, therefore, gave all available monies–nearly $13,000--to supply the preemptive strike to destroy Major Ferguson and his Loyalists.

One typical plucky Irish frontiersmen among Colonel Shelby's warriors was John Crockett, who had been born in Ireland. He originally hailed from the beautiful region along the south coast of Ireland near the sheltered blue waters surrounded by high rocky ridges, the elongated and majestic Bantry Bay. He would be the future father of David

Crockett, the Tennessee Congressman, who was destined to be killed by Mexicans at the Alamo on March 6, 1836, after a good many Irish and Scotch-Irish had settled the northern Mexican province known as Texas and fought to win Texas independence from another centralized power and Mother Country, the Republic of Mexico. John's father and David Crockett's grandfather was a settler of Carter's Valley, when killed by a Creek war party during the American Revolution.

Another fiery Ireland-born soldier from the west side of the mountains was Captain James Dysart, who would be wounded at Kings Mountain. He had been born in County Donegal in northern Ireland. As a teenager, he migrated from Ulster Province to Philadelphia, before pushing on to the wilderness of the Holston River country. A legendary "Long Hunter, " the Irishman was one of the early explorers of not only Tennessee, but also of the Kentucky bluegrass country.

Hundreds of highly-motivated "overmountain" men, with tomahawks and long rifles gathered at Sycamore Shoals on the muster day, September 25. The next day, they planned to depart. Assembling with his followers, one of the most respected members of the frontier communities on the west side of the Blue Ridge was a man of God. He heightened the righteous fervor among these Irish and Scotch-Irish frontiersmen at Sycamore Shoals now surrounded by trees now draped in early fall colors.. Reverend Samuel Doak was a spiritual and community leader among the frontiersmen from the west side of the Blue Ridge. While journeying across the Atlantic, Doak's Irish immigrant parents had been married on the sailing ship that brought them from Ireland to America.

On a balmy morning of September 26, 1780 and surrounded by dark green forests just starting to take on the lighter hues of early fall, especially the towering sycamores along the river bottoms, Reverend Doak prepared to present his most memorable religious service, despite this was a

Tuesday instead of Sunday. While the westerners stood with heads bowed and leaned on their muskets, he stood atop a big stump at Sycamore Shoals. Then, the Scotch-Irish reverend knew that he had to inspire the hundreds of frontiersmen with a religious zeal, just before they rode off on this preemptive strike expedition rode off to confront Ferguson and to end the threat to the western settlements. Reverend Doak, therefore, reflected upon the ancient "Macedonian call being heard in the east by people in desperate need."

Here, in the morning light of early autumn, he bestowed a spiritual blessing upon around 600 well-armed frontiersmen, equipped with long rifles, scalping knives, and tomahawks, before they embarked. Reverend Doak, who spoke ancient Hebrew as in the days of the Old Testament, reminded his frontier "shirt men," named for their long hunting shirts of deerskin, that this was a righteous struggle. The Presbyterian man of God emphasized how this fight was all about freedom, reminding them that their struggle was as holy as that of the Israelites against their oppressors, the Egyptians and Romans.

More specifically, Reverend Doak's emotional sermon reminded the western frontiersmen of the inspiring example of Gideon's successful uprising against the Midianites. Wishing to maintain the right for his followers of the Watauga settlements to worship in the Presbyterian faith free of the influence of the Anglican Church, Reverend Doak implored these frontiersmen who had gathered at Sycamore Shoals to defend the land they loved with an inspirational invocation: "Let that be your battle cry: the sword of the Lord and of Gideon." Then, these "sturdy, Scotch-Irish Presbyterians around him, clothed in their tidy hunting-shirts, and leaning upon their rifles in an attitude of respectful attention, shouted in patriotic acclaim: 'The sword of the Lord and our Gideons!'."

In total, nearly 900 tough fighting men from the

Carolinas, Virginia, and what would become Tennessee and from both sides of the mountains, "without any order from the executives of our different States" were all united in a great gathering of the frontier clans in the Celtic-Gaelic tradition of defending the homeland against an invader, from the ancient Romans to the imperialistic British. Most of these frontiersmen who united at Sycamore Shoals were Irish and Scotch-Irish. The Gaelic-Celtic warriors from the westernmost settlements would be eventually join with men from the east side of the mountains, including Irish commanders like Captain James McCall of the South Carolina Piedmont and his band of followers, and Joseph McJunkin, who was another Scotch-Irish leader of the Palmetto State. Also volunteers poured forth from the Irish Settlement near Fair Forest Creek in the South Carolina Piedmont. This settlement was so thoroughly Celtic that it was known at the time simply as Ireland.

But the majority of the Irish and Scotch-Irish of this expeditionary force hailed from the west side of the Smoky Mountains. These were the Watauga, Clinch, Nolachucky and Holston River valley riflemen, whose skills were well known. When they rode east to meet Major Ferguson and his Loyalists, they left their isolated frontier settlements and families vulnerable to Cherokee raids in their absence: a necessary risk that had to be taken. These frontiersmen already knew well of the horrors of frontier warfare, after battling Indians for decades.

One of those veteran commanders who led a regiment at Kings Mountain was Lieutenant Colonel James Hawthorn. Like so many of his men, Hawthorn had been born in Ireland. The family had migrated from County Armagh, Ireland, to the South Carolina frontier, where the twelve-year old, his mother, and two sisters were captured by Indians. Hawthorn was the only survivor of what became a living nightmare. The young man witnessed the killing of not only his mother but also his two sisters by their Native American captors. After his release from captivity, Hawthorn became a South Carolina blacksmith, and then a hard-fighting militia leader.

After crossing the mountains, the frontiersmen were reinforced by North Carolina militia under Colonel Benjamin Cleveland, a veteran Indian fighter, and Major Joseph Winston. Soon the patriot ranks were swelled to nearly 1,500 men, after small bands of partisans of Georgia, South Carolina, and North Carolina guerrillas who had been battling in the Piedmont, likewise rallied to the ad hoc western army of frontiersmen. And now a new leader had to be chosen to command this large body of troops from both sides of the mountains.

In the same time-honored tradition as the ancient warrior of Irish clans picking their own chieftain to defend their homeland of Ireland, these westerners also chose their own warrior leader, Colonel Campbell. He was a revered Celtic-Gaelic chieftain, who had won the respect of not only his Virginians but also the men from the most remote western frontier in America. With typical English contempt for alleged inferiors of the lower classes, these hardy frontiersmen were viewed by the British as nothing more than "Backwater Barbarians," and "a set of mongrels."

Ironically, this perception was almost the identical English view of the native people of Ireland, especially Catholics, for centuries. Such negative stereotypes served as a convenient justification for British oppression and persecution in a bloody, so-called "civilizing" mission by way of the sword on both sides of the Atlantic. And no more was more guilty of underestimating these hardy frontiersmen than Major Ferguson, who viewed the colonists in arms with the utmost contempt.

Meanwhile, after pushing through the Blue Ridge mountain gaps, the westerners continued their pursuit of Ferguson ever-southeast amid the beautiful autumn foliage.

With vengeance on their minds, Campbell's men continued to close-in on their quarry. Finally, on October 5, Colonel Campbell gained intelligence that Major Ferguson's troops were approaching the high ground of Kings Mountain. These frontiersmen knew that if Ferguson made a stand on the commanding mountaintop, then some hard fighting lay in store for them.

Ironically, however, because Ferguson so thoroughly underestimated the fighting capabilities of this frontier army of mostly Irish and Scotch-Irish frontiersmen from the river valleys of the Watauga, Yadkin, Nolichunky, Clinch, Holston, and Catawba, he quite casually prepared to make a defensive stand atop Kings Mountain upon learning that "the Campbells were coming."

An overconfident Major Ferguson now awaited the arrival of Campbell's force to begin the fray. He wanted to make a name for himself, knowing that a decisive victory over this frontier "rabble" would win him glory, promotion, and fame in an increasingly unglamourous war in the South. Besides awaiting for reinforcements from Lord Cornwallis that would not be forthcoming, he was eager to demonstrate what his finely-drilled American Loyalist soldiers could accomplish against such a unruly band of backwoods farmers and "white savages."

Ferguson, therefore, made his stand on the most dominant high ground near the North Carolina-South Carolina border, Kings Mountain. This ill-advised decision was made after rejecting the sound concept of prudently retiring toward the safety of Charlotte to rejoin Lord Cornwallis's main force only around thirty miles distant. On his rocky, high ground perch covered in dense hardwood forest, Major Ferguson all but dared the fast-approaching Blue Ridge frontiersmen and Southern militiamen to attack his disciplined soldiers. Consequently, the Scottish leader well-positioned his Loyalist troops along the lengthy ridgeline of Kings Mountain, that was heavily timbered except on the top. Ferguson did not even bother to throw up a light breastwork or order the digging of trenches on the hilltop, however.

In reality, Ferguson's decision to take a defensive position on Kings Mountain in northern South Carolina and just below the North Carolina line sealed the fate of his American Loyalists from New York and New Jersey in scarlet-colored uniforms and his Southern Loyalist militiamen. However, Major Ferguson believed that he and his 800-1,000 men could easily beat the Americans, especially if reinforcements arrived in time from Lord Cornwallis. After all, he had immense pride and confidence in his well-trained soldiers of the Queen's Rangers, the King's American Rangers, and the New Jersey Volunteers. Just before the battle, he widely boasted how "all the Rebels from hell could not drive him from" Kings Mountain. He would soon have the opportunity to prove his boast.

All the while, Colonel Campbell's troops continued their pursuit with a determination to catch Ferguson and his Tories, before they came to their senses and slipped away from Kings Mountain. Colonel Shelby, therefore, had earlyed urged a forced push with the best men on the freshest horses to catch Major Ferguson before he escaped On nearing Kings Mountain, which rose about sixty feet from the surrounding and generally rolling landscape of the Piedmont, after riding both day and night, the so-called "Back Water men," as Major Ferguson contemptuously called them because they lived beyond of sources of the rivers that flowed eastward, made final preparations to meet the enemy. Here, about a mile from Kings Mountain, they hitched their horses to trees and prepared to advance on foot in stealthy fashion.

Most important, the approach of Campbell's men had not been detected. Frontier leaders divided the men into four columns. With stealth, these assault columns then advanced through the woods toward Kings Mountain and then took assigned positions around Ferguson's hilltop perch. Major Ferguson was shocked when the first alerted Tories fired their first shots at the encroaching "over mountain men," warning him to the danger already at his doorstep. Ferguson's shock was complete. Not only the Indian-style advance through the forest but also Ferguson's lack of adequate security measures ensured that he was caught totally by surprise.

Eager for a fight, Campbell's men were instructed in typical frontier fashion to "Let each one of you be your own officer, and do the very best you can, taking every care you can of yourselves, and availing yourselves of every advantage that chance may throw in your way [and] shelter yourselves [in the timber], and give them Indian play; advance from tree to tree, pressing the enemy and killing and disabling all you can."

In his shirt-sleeves and looking not unlike a Celtic-Gaelic clan leader from ancient times on the Green Isle, Colonel Campbell implored his men onward just after 3 o'clock on this hot afternoon of October 7, 1780 in northern South Carolina: "Here they are, my brave boys; shout like hell, and fight like devils!" As Major Ferguson had anticipated and in the traditional Celtic style of warfare, the frontiersmen of mostly Irish and Scotch-Irish descent immediately launched an attack upon ascertaining that Ferguson and his troops were waiting for them atop Kings Mountain, now tinged in the bright colors of early autumn.

In typical Celtic-Gaelic fashion, the Irish and Scotch-Irish swarmed up the wooded, steep, and rocky slopes of Kings Mountain with clannish war cries of old Ireland. Fighting Indian style up the steep slopes, the frontiersmen, with long hair and looking almost like ancient Celtic-Gaelic ancestors, closed-in on Major Ferguson's command on the mountaintop.

Ferguson and his Loyalists now realized they were in serious trouble, when their heard the shrill Celtic-Gaelic war-cries of "the damned yelling boys!" Indeed, while the attackers possessed the advantage of assaulting uphill through heavy timber that screened their approach, Ferguson's troops were exposed on the open, clear ground atop Kings Mountain. The last order that the Scotch-Irish frontiersmen had received from their no-nonsense Celtic-Gaelic leader, Colonel Campbell, was for every soldier "to fight till he dies!"

Deadly marksmanship from the long rifles cut down leading officers among Major Ferguson's force on the bare crest of Kings Mountain, which offered a good field of fire. Meanwhile, Campbell's attackers possessed the advantage of fighting from behind the cover of trees. As if on an European battleground, Ferguson made the mistake of attempting to defend Kings Mountain with the tactical offensive and the bayonet. He launched one bayonet attack after another down the slopes, as if hoping to scare away the frontier marksmen, who could not be intimated and merely took cover and blasted away from behind trees and rocks. For sometime, charge and counter-charge surged back and forth along the slopes of Kings Mountain.

When Major Ferguson was hit by multiple bullets and killed while attempting to lead an attempt to break through the constricting swarms of the steadily advancing frontiersmen, Loyalist resistance finally collapsed. One Scotch-Irish rifleman claimed that a shot from his long rifle, nicknamed "Sweet Lips," knocked Ferguson off his horse. After suffering heavy losses in killed and wounded of around 300 men, surrounded by howling frontiersmen, and with no chance to escape, the Loyalists surrendered to their fellow Americans. One disgruntled Loyalist described the humiliating defeat that was as thorough as it was swift: "the cursed rebels [had] killed and took us every soul" on this decisive fall day.

In only a hour of bitter fighting, the "shirt men" won an improbable victory amid the dense woodlands and slopes of Kings Mountain. With the loss of less than 100 men, they had eliminated Ferguson and his Loyalists in one swift stroke. Intoxicated by their victory, the frontiersmen celebrated their amazing success, thanks to a gathering of the Celtic-Gaelic clans and a heavy reliance upon Indian and frontier tactics, with a chorus of three cheers, "Hurrah for Liberty" that rang across the body-strewn slopes of Kings Mountain.

But there was precious little time for celebration. All the while, the victors of Kings Mountain prayed that the Cherokee had not descended upon their vulnerable western settlements and their families during their two-week absence. After all, they were now more than a hundred miles from the isolated homeland on the other side of the mountains.

In overall strategic terms, the patriot victory at Kings Mountain was the first serious setback of General Cornwallis' ambitious strategy to conquer the entire South. More than 1,000 provincial regulars and Tory militiamen were either killed, wounded, or captured. The defeat of the best trained and largest concentration of armed Loyalists in the South ended the British dream of mobilizing a vast Loyalist Army to crush the revolution in the South. The left wing of Lord Cornwallis' Army had been destroyed. Most important in overall strategic terms, the soil of North Carolina was swept clean of British troops by the dramatic victory at Kings Mountain, deflating the morale of both the British and their American Loyalist allies alike. The stunning success unexpectedly reaped by a ghost army of western frontiersmen and ragtag Southern militia, that had seemingly emerged out of thin air, was largely won by mostly Irish and Scotch-Irish warriors. Defeated Loyalists were shocked by the sight of the victors from the western frontier:

"the most powerful men ever beheld, tall, rawboned and sinewy," wrote one of the vanquished officers in Ferguson's command.

Most significant, this old formula of a traditional Celtic-Gaelic gathering of the clans as in Ireland of old against the English invaders, and more recently Native Americans, on their own initiative and fighting on their own hook without government authority or approval had been the key to victory at Kings Mountain. After all and like Irish revolutionaries for centuries against the English interlopers, without state or national orders, support, or directives, these mostly Scotch-Irish soldiers had organized themselves on their own, relied upon their own resources, and rallied around their community leaders, like the ancient Irish kings, to repel an invader that threatened homes and families.

Relying upon their own initiative to launch a long-distance expedition over the mountains to unleash a preemptive strike to catch an opponent by surprise, this rough-hewn, untrained band of mostly Celtic-Gaelic warriors from the western frontier decisively defeated Cornwallis' top lieutenant and some of the finest troops in his highly-professional army, even after they had chosen to defend the highest and most commanding ground in the area.

Clearly, Major Ferguson's downfall at Kings Mountain was due primarily to the fact that he had so thoroughly underestimated not only the numbers and fighting qualities of the "over mountain men," but also how an ancient Celtic-Gaelic gathering of the clans could quickly create manufacture a frontier army from scratch. Indeed, in the words of Mark Boatner, III, a "large number of small units rallied quickly, achieved unity of command, and destroyed their enemy in a remarkably businesslike manner." Most significant, for the Scotch-Irish and Irish frontiersmen of the South and their veteran Celtic-Gaelic leaders, this was their finest and "greatest hour."

Most important, this surprising patriot victory at Kings Mountain played a key role in paving the way to the final drama at Yorktown and Cornwallis' surrender. Much like the inspirational affect of General Washington's victory at Trenton in late December 1776, American confidence was lifted across the colonies, especially in the South where patriot fortunes had faltered badly, raising new hopes for success and invigorating the patriot cause. While the Loyalists of the South began to lose hope and turn away from the Crown, the patriots were rejuvenated by the stunning victory at Kings Mountain. Quite simply, American success at Kings Mountain was the key turning point of the American Revolution in the South.

In a letter, for instance, an elated General Washington wrote how the unexpected victory at Kings Mountain demonstrated the "proof of the spirit and resources of the country." A distinctive Celtic-Gaelic fighting spirit and the dark legacies of the Irish past had played key roles in leading to the remarkable success of the Irish and Scotch-Irish frontiersmen and the Southern militiamen at Kings Mountain.

The commander of the Irish Volunteers, a stunned Lord Rawdon, as revealed in a letter to Lord Cornwallis, could hardly believe that the swift vanquishing of Ferguson's well-equipped forces at Kings Mountain had been achieved by a band of nondescript western frontiersmen, who hailed from the remote far reaches of the "Nolachucki [sic] and other settlements beyond the mountains, whose very names had been unknown to us." Without exaggeration, historian Walter Edgar concluded how the mass "migration of predominantly Scots-Irish [had] transformed the lower South and, in the final analysis, was key to America's triumph over Great Britain in the Revolution." And this undeniable reality was convincingly demonstrated by the amazing Irish and the Scotch-Irish success at Kings Mountain.

More than any other single factor, the dramatic victory at Kings Mountain was the result of the spontaneous rising of the Irish and Scotch-Irish clans to defend home and family. As Sir Henry Clinton lamented Major Ferguson's defeat at Kings Mountain, this was "an event which was immediately productive of the worst consequences to the King's affairs in South Carolina, and unhappily the first link in the chain of evils that followed in regular succession until they at last ended in the loss of America."

The contributions of the mostly Irish and Scotch-Irish from the remote frontier settlements on the west side of the mountains in vanquishing both the Indians and their British allies, especially at Kings Mountain, not only played an important role in winning the American Revolution, but also were instrumental in securing the trans-Appalachian West for a new nation conceived in revolution.

Chapter V: A Vengeful Irishman's Tactical Masterpiece at the Cowpens on January 17, 1781

The most brilliant, innovative, and original tactical plan of battle on either side during the American Revolution was conceived by Ireland-born General Daniel Morgan. He was the son of Irish immigrants from County Derry in northern Ireland. He, therefore, has been described as a "Derryman." Born in 1736, Morgan was a native of Ballinascreen, County Derry, Ireland, and a devout Presbyterian. Like so many other Scotch-Irish soldiers in America, Morgan fought as if he was waging a holy war to vanquish the British invaders of his native homeland on the Atlantic's other side.

Morgan's unmatched tactical masterpiece at Cowpens, South Carolina, brought a much-needed victory in the war in the South. The tactical skill that General Morgan demonstrated in cleverly adapting distinctive American fighting strengths and native ways of fighting in America's woodlands against Native Americans to traditional Eighteenth Century European tactics allowed him to reap a dramatic success at the battle of Cowpens on January 17, 1781. Not a better example of innovative and imaginative tactics developed largely from the lessons learned from the new realities of warfare in America and the frontier experience can be found in the American Revolution than with Morgan's remarkable victory at the Cowpens.

A dynamic figure from the western frontier of the Valley of Virginia, the Ireland-born Morgan was as unorthodox as he was impressive as a natural leader. Hating nothing more than pretense and formality, especially military protocol, Morgan, even as a general, always remained as homespun and accessible to his men as possible. But this was only an outside appearance and facade.

Inside his plain and roughhewn exterior lay a brilliant general and tactical genius. Not unlike Ireland-born General Andrew Jackson during the War of 1812, Morgan's plainness and simplicity was one secret of his success in commanding the ever-individualist American soldiers. For General Morgan, such a command style was only natural, stemming from his experience as not only an Irishman but also as a Virginia backwoodsman.

A product of two equally harsh, unforgiving environments, ever-volatile Ireland and Virginia's western frontier, Morgan was tough and hard-as-nails by the war's beginning. But the Irishman was also sensitive to the needs of his men, who looked upon Morgan as a father figure. In part reflecting his County Derry, Ireland, upbringing and a well-known Celtic-Gaelic temperament, he possessed a hot Irish temper. For instance, Morgan was known for resorting to his fists in manners of honor, and also for defying and even physically battling high-ranking officers–British or American–both before and during the American Revolution.

During the French and Indian War, Morgan's knocking down of an autocratic British officer resulted in a punishment of 500 lashes that he would never forget. Like Jackson in receiving the slash across the forehead by a British officer's saber as a young South Carolina revolutionary, this punishment left Morgan with a lifelong hatred for the British: a factor that in part led to the creation of one of America's finest Continental generals. Despite his lofty rank, the Irishman of humble origins called himself the "Old Wagoner." He was yet proud of his once lowly status while serving with a British Army: an absolute delight to his admiring Continental soldiers, especially lower class Scotch-Irish and immigrant Irish. Morgan's sobriquet stemmed from his days as a civilian teamster for the British Army during the Seven Years' War.

Like so many other of his fellow Celtic-Gaelic

113

countrymen, the ever-restless Irishman had migrated south and down the Great Wagon Road from Pennsylvania to the Winchester, Frederick County, Virginia, area, where so many Irish and Scotch-Irish had settled in virgin land, as a young man. From the beginning, Morgan was a natural frontiersman. He often wore Indian and frontier clothes, and this backwoods tradition continued during his early service in the American Revolution.

Like General Washington, he was also a Virginia slave-owner. But unlike this wealthy planter in the Virginia tidewater along the Potomac River, Morgan was a common yeoman farmer of the western frontier. This County Derry Irishman, therefore, owned only a few slaves in farming the land, while Washington owned hundreds of slaves at his sprawling Mount Vernon plantation.

By the time of the American Revolution, Morgan was a product of the untamed wilderness region of western frontier of Maryland, Pennsylvania, and Virginia. Because of both his Irish and western frontier background, he always remained a soldiers' general. Both on campaign and off, he treated his men with a kindness that bordered on tenderness. Even the lowly privates, who he called "my dear boys," were treated by Morgan as equals and worthy of respect: characteristics born of both the Irish and frontier experience.

These were distinctive Morgan characteristics that the vast majority of other generals, including the aloof, patrician General Washington, would not emulate. In this simplistic way, Morgan gained more confidence and respect among his men, paying dividends during the climactic showdown at Cowpens.

Another factor explaining General Morgan's success as a commander was his experience in the French and Indian Wars, including the clashes with Native Americans on the remote Virginia frontier. The hard-fighting Morgan earned distinction as a savvy Virginia Ranger on the western frontier, and as a daring captain leading a militia company of his Frederick County, Virginia, neighbors, many of whom were Irish and Scotch-Irish, before the American Revolution's beginning. He not only led troops in Pontiac's War, but also battled Shawnee, Delaware warriors and their allies in the struggle for possession of the Ohio Valley in 1774.

When the Continental Congress requested Maryland, Pennsylvania, and Virginia to furnish volunteer companies of frontier riflemen for service in June 1775, Morgan was elected captain of a crack rifle company from western Virginia. Inspired by the concept of fighting for their freedom like their Irish ancestors on the Emerald Isle, these western frontiersmen, whom a large percentage were Irish and Scotch-Irish, wore the motto of "Liberty or Death" across the breast of their frontier hunting shirts.

During an arduous 600-mile, 21-day journey north at a rapid pace and even before receiving orders to march from the Continental Congress, Captain Morgan on his own led nearly 100 Virginia riflemen of Frederick County, Virginia, to join the forming patriot army at Cambridge, Massachusetts, just outside British-held Boston, during 1775's summer. Dressed in Native American costume, including moccasins, Indian leggings, and carrying tomahawks, Morgan and his western frontiersmen completed the lengthy march in record time of only three weeks. The sight of Morgan and his rugged westerners shocked the sensibilities of the more refined New Englanders. So throughly Celtic-Gaelic were the ranks of Captain Morgan's rifle company that they have been described as "these wonderful Irish riflemen." Indeed, Morgan's individualistic soldiers from the western frontier of Virginia were "in great part Ulster in background . . . . "

The lethal capabilities of Morgan's westerners was demonstrated as soon as they joined General Washington's

Army. With deadly efficiency, Morgan's frontiersmen immediately began to methodically pick off British soldiers, especially finely-uniformed officers, with long distance shots from their long rifles. So deadly was the skill of Morgan's sharpshooting Virginians that Ireland-born Edmund Burke proclaimed in the House of Parliament in London how: "Your officers are swept off by the rifles if they but show their noses!"

After a brief service with General Washington's Army, Captain Morgan and his riflemen then joined the expeditionary force of Colonel Benedict Arnold of Connecticut. Arnold gave Captain Morgan, who continued to wear Indian costume in the frontier tradition, command of three rifle companies for their greatest challenge to date, the invasion of Canada. Colonel Arnold commanded one wing of the American invasion force of Canada. The other wing was led by Ireland-born General Richard Montgomery, who would take overall command when the two forces united.

Morgan's leadership skills rose to the fore during the arduous 350-mile march north through the rugged Maine wilderness to Canada. Displaying outstanding leadership ability, matched only by Arnold's equally inspiring example, during one of the difficult marches in American history, Morgan played a key role in keeping the Kennebec column intact during its difficult sojourn through the wilderness. In a letter, one Pennsylvania soldier marveled at Morgan's leadership abilities. He wrote how the many challenges of the epic wilderness march were "left to the energy of Morgan's mind, and he conquered."

After the columns of Colonel Arnold and Ireland-born General Richard Montgomery united, the offensive effort to capture Quebec was launched in a blinding snowstorm on December's last day. Arnold and Morgan led the attack into Quebec's Lower Town from the north, while Montgomery's column struck the Lower Town from the south. Disaster soon resulted, however, when General Montgomery was killed early in the attack and the southern column was repulsed, ending the desperate bid to capture Quebec in this sector.

After Arnold was cut down by a blast of cannon fire like General Montgomery who had fallen before him, Morgan took charge of the survivors to continue the attack through the swirling snowstorm. In a forlorn hope against the odds and believing correctly that a good chance for success yet remained, Morgan led his column of attackers forward in a desperate bid to capture Quebec on his own. With Arnold down and despite only holding a captain's rank, Morgan now acted as the commanding officer. Incredibly, Morgan continued to implore his men onward through the blinding snow, even though the two top American leaders had been cut down.

Captain Morgan's repeated efforts to push forward with only relatively few men in one last effort to yet win the day awed the British. Hundreds of rallied British troops descended upon Morgan and his doomed band of half-frozen survivors to entrap them, forcing their surrender. However, a typically-defiant Morgan refused to surrender his sword to a British officer, risking death rather than submit and suffer the humiliation. Even though all other Americans had surrendered, Morgan hotly replied with a threat of his own to a British officer's demand to hand over his sword, "Come take it if you dare!" In a final defiant act that comforted his Irish soul, he finally handed his saber to a nearby Catholic priest instead of a hated British soldier, which he simply refused to do, even if it meant death. Upon handing over his sword to the surprised priest and even in defeat, a proud Morgan swore with typical Irish defiance: "No scoundrel of these [British] cowards shall take it out of my hands." Clearly, Morgan had neither forgotten or forgiven the hundreds of lashes that he had received as a younger man.

Against seemingly all chances for success, Morgan had narrowly missed capturing Quebec, despite the fall of both Montgomery and Arnold. Caused by fellow officers "who were contemptuous of this rough frontiersmen,"the ever-aggressive Irishman had agreed to a fatal delay in the hope that Arnold's column–which was not coming--would arrive for an united offensive effort to yet win the day. But in fact, if "Morgan's advice had been followed . . . he might have been successful and the city might have fallen." If so, then not only Quebec, but also Canada might well have become the Fourteenth Colony. Indeed, the feisty Irishman named Morgan had almost accomplished the impossible in the snowy streets of Quebec.

Though thwarted in the ill-fated bid to capture Quebec in the depths of a severe snowstorm, Morgan and his riflemen were only beginning to play leading roles in major battles of the American Revolution. Despite only holding a captain's rank, Morgan's inspiring performance during the wilderness march to Canada and during the audacious attack on Quebec gained widespread recognition for the roughhewn Virginian. For example, when General Washington wrote to John Hancock, who was of Ireland-born parents and the president of the Continental Congress, and proposed that the recently exchanged Morgan be given command of the army's newly proposed rifle regiment, Hancock was most receptive to the idea. With satisfaction, he, therefore, wrote back to General Washington, emphasizing how the rifle regiment would be "kept for Mr. Morgan."

After exchange in late 1776, Morgan's longtime ambitions were finally realized when he was given command of the Eleventh Virginia Continental Regiment. But recruitment languished and other internal and external problems developed for Colonel Morgan's fledgling regiment. Therefore, in the winter of 1777, General Washington ordered Morgan to recruit a specially created corps of light infantry, or frontier sharpshooters, consisting of carefully chosen Continental troops, including frontiersmen from the Eleventh Virginia.

Originally, Morgan's unit was to have been a Virginia rifle corps, but he found it necessary to fill out the ranks with riflemen from the frontiers of western and southern Pennsylvania, including the Cumberland Valley, and western Maryland. To qualify for entry into the new crack rifle corps, these frontiersmen had to meet high standards of marksmanship. Many Irish and Scotch-Irish riflemen who enlisted in Morgan's rifle corps were French and Indian War veterans. Nearly one-half of Morgan's rifle corps–46 percent–were either born in Ireland or descended from Irish parents, while the Scotch-Irish made-up the second highest percentage.

For instance, in the ranks of Captain Michael Simpson's company of Colonel Morgan's rifle corps were young Irishmen and Scotch-Irish like Private Timothy Murphy, Sergeant Jonathan McMahon, Corporal John Kelly, Corporal John Ryan, Private Patrick McCaw, Private John McCreerly, and Private John McKinney. Hatred of the British and lethal proficiency with the long rifle ensured that these mostly Irish and Scotch-Irish warriors of Colonel Morgan's rifle corps were "the most fatal widow-and-orphan makers in the world," lamented a British reporter in a London newspaper.

With considerable skill, Colonel Morgan commanded the veteran sharpshooters of his rifle corps of eight companies from the spring of 1777 to July of 1778. Repeatedly, Morgan and his unit served as the invaluable eyes and ears of Washington's Continental Army. Morgan and his men were ideal troops for successfully conducting raids and engaging in guerrilla warfare in the frontier tradition. In essence, Morgan and his frontiersmen were employed repeatedly as Washington's valued frontier "rangers." These were identical roles that many of these same soldiers, including Morgan himself, had played during the long and bloody years of the French and Indian War. In Washington's revealing words which did not exaggerate the importance of Morgan and his men: "This corps I have great dependence on . . . ." But this written statement by General Washington was in fact an understatement.

Colonel Morgan and his rifle corps saw their finest day during the Saratoga campaign of 1777. Washington reluctantly dispatched 400 soldiers of his elite rifle corps under Morgan to reinforce General Horatio Gates and his northern army to thwart the advance of General John Burgoyne's Army of British, Tories, Germans, and Indians from Canada. This powerful British Army descended south down the Hudson River, marching through the wilderness of upper New York virtually unopposed. Burgoyne's Army pushed south with the intention of linking with General Henry Clinton's British Army, if dispatched in time from New York City, at Albany, New York. England's overall strategic objective of cutting New England off from the rest of the colonies was a wise strategic plan calculated upon the concept of divide and conquer to subjugate the northern colonies.

To meet this challenge, Washington would depend a great deal upon Colonel Morgan and his frontier riflemen. In General Washington's opinion, "I know of no Corps so likely to check [General Burgoyne's advance] in proportion to their number" than Morgan and his rifle corps. Colonel Morgan's riflemen became the elite corps of the northern army, serving in both offensive and defensive roles against the British and Hessians. This fine "regiment of Irish sharpshooters" included reliable soldiers like Lieutenant Colonel Richard Butler of Kilkenny, Ireland, and his brother Pierce Butler, who commanded a rifle company.

Armed with their deadly long rifles, Morgan's

frontiersmen, of mostly Irish and Scotch-Irish descent, not only played a leading role in causing many of General Burgoyne's Indian allies to desert but also wrecked havoc on the elite British regulars. Despite being outnumbered, Morgan and his men demonstrated offensive capabilities and inflicted high casualties upon General Burgoyne's forces by relying on headlong attack, flank maneuvers, and lethal sharpshooting throughout the Saratoga campaign, especially during the two battles of Saratoga on September 19 and October 7, 1777. Fighting from the cover of trees like Native Americans and maneuvering to the shrill signals of Morgan's turkey call that could be heard above the battle's roar, the sharpshooters decimated the British officers corps. Morgan's riflemen deflated British morale with the long distance shots that struck down so many of General Burgoyne's officers, reminding them that death could strike unexpectedly at almost anytime.

Not only shooting British officers off their horses, these crack riflemen also cut to pieces the exposed British artillery crews, which were especially vulnerable in the open fields of early autumn along the Hudson. Such decimation reduced the British Army's effectiveness during the clashes at Freeman's Farm during one of the war's most decisive campaigns. Throughout September and early days of October, Colonel Morgan's men harassed the British day and night, shattering the once unsurmountable confidence of General Burgoyne's troops with their lethal marksmanship.

One of the hardest-fighting Irishmen and experienced Indian fighters of Morgan's rifle corps, who won widespread fame at the battle of Saratoga was rifleman Timothy Murphy. Born in 1751, the young frontiersman hailed from the Irish community of the Delaware River Gap, before his Irish immigrant family moved to the Shamokin Flats of Pennsylvania. The Murphy family later moved to the Wyoming Valley of Pennsylvania. In June 1775, Murphy

121

and his brother, John, enlisted in a volunteer company from Northumberland County, Pennsylvania. After gaining a good deal of military experience from the siege of Boston to the New Jersey campaign, he then joined Morgan's riflemen in the summer of 1777.

Calling for the expert marksmanship of one of "my best shots," Colonel Morgan ordered Private Murphy, an illiterate but savvy frontiersmen, up a tall tree for the specific purpose of shooting down a particularly courageous British officer mounted on a grey horse during the second battle of Saratoga on October 7. Inspiring his troops by his own bravery, this targeted officer was none other than General Simon Fraser, second in command in General Burgoyne's Army. He was a Scottish warrior widely known for his fearlessness and leadership ability both on and off the battlefield. With a long-distance shot from his trusty long rifle, Murphy fatally cut down not only General Fraser at a distance of 300 yards but also Sir Francis Clarke on October 7, helping to seal the decisive American victory at Saratoga that eventually secured the all-important French Alliance from Paris.

Born in New Jersey in 1751 and a former member of the Northumberland County Riflemen of Pennsylvania and Colonel Thompson's Rifle Battalion, Murphy had qualified for enlistment in Colonel Morgan's rifle corps in July 1777, after demonstrating his expertise with his small caliber long rifle that could knock down a target at several hundred yards. Like so many of Morgan's riflemen, Murphy was the son of Irish parents who had recently migrated across the Atlantic from the green fields and rolling hills of County Donegal in northern Ireland.

Murphy's humble roots beguiled the important role that he played at Saratoga: a rare case of a lowly enlisted man having a dramatic impact on a major battle and a campaign. The death of Burgoyne's second in command was yet another factor that led to British defeat at the decisive battle of

Saratoga. Morgan was convinced that the vital role that his frontier riflemen played at Saratoga "settled the business" in favor of General Gates and his northern army.

In more than meeting his match at Saratoga, General Burgoyne had fought on his own without any real hope of assistance from General Clinton's British Army at New York City. General Burgoyne's surrender came on October 17, 1777 at Saratoga. As no other troops at Saratoga, Colonel Morgan and his riflemen had a large role in forcing that capitulation. A grateful Washington bestowed a fine tribute upon Morgan and his frontier riflemen. He praised this "intrepid corps [and] for their gallant behaviour [sic]" at Saratoga. Throughout the Continental Army, Morgan's riflemen became known as "the pride of Washington," and for good reason.

One of Morgan's dependable top lieutenants who saw service at Saratoga with his rifle corps was Lieutenant Colonel Richard Butler of Pennsylvania. He was born in St. Bridget's Parish, Dublin, Ireland, on July 1, 1743, and settled in the Cumberland Valley of Pennsylvania like so many other Irish and Scotch-Irish pioneers. Butler gained experience not only as an Indian trader but also as the Fifth Pennsylvania Regiment's colonel, before joining Colonel Morgan's rifle corps. He then fought as a lieutenant colonel at Saratoga, where he performed with distinction.

Yet another hard-fighting Butler served with Morgan's famed rifle corps, Pierce Butler. The son of Thomas Butler of Kilkenny, Ireland, he was one of five brothers from Pennsylvania's beautiful Cumberland Valley. These brothers fought against the British with the tenacity of their Irish ancestors, who had battled the English for so long in Ireland.

Washington's faith in General Morgan was fully reciprocated again and again. When the conspiracy to ruin Washington's reputation and dispose him as commander-in-chief was underway during the winter of 1777-1778, General

Morgan was incensed by the widespread betrayals. When he encountered an anti-Washington Richard Peters, the secretary of the Board of War, he lost his Irish temper and demonstrated that his Celtic-Gaelic fighting spirit was as vibrant off the battlefield as on it. Morgan flew into a rage at the mere sight of Peters. In no uncertain terms, the Irishman then denounced him for his part in the devious scheme to destroy Washington's reputation. When Peters denied that such a anti-Washington conspiracy existed, Morgan then asked Peters if he was calling him a liar. At last, the "terrified Peters realized this was the prelude to a challenge to a duel . . . but two days later, he was still shaking when he described the encounter to a friend."

Meanwhile, British strategists turned their ambitions southward after acquiescing to stalemate in the north and the failure to vanquish General Washington's Army and the humiliating loss of an entire British army at Saratoga, New York. This new offensive strategy for conquering the South paid both immediate and high dividends. British efforts gained much of the South, Georgia and South Carolina, and major seaports, such as Savannah, Georgia, and Charleston, South Carolina, for the Crown by early 1781.

General Nathaniel Greene's small patriot army was the largest organized American force capable of offering resistance, after General Gates's disastrous defeat at Camden, South Carolina, in mid-August 1780: ironically a command gained by Gates for his Saratoga success, which Morgan and General Arnold had done more tactically to accomplish than "Granny" Gates. After the Camden fiasco, the overall British commander in the South, who was England's most energetic and capable leader, General Cornwallis, planned to invade and conquer North Carolina.

First, however, Lord Cornwallis prepared to seek out and destroy General Greene's forces, especially Morgan's fast-moving task force of light infantry and dragoons that had been detached from Greene's army and was operating in his rear. As a good commander who ignored the temptation to understatement the abilities of this "Old Wagoner" like so many other British commanders, Cornwallis understood that this Irishman posed no ordinary threat. Indeed, Morgan's reputation from military exploits in the snowy streets of Quebec and in Saratoga's dark forests had preceded him. Much to his credit, the haughty Lord Cornwallis accorded a rare amount of respect for an Irish commander, by taking Morgan seriously as a commander. In addition, he realized that Morgan had to be eliminated before he could carry-out his strategic plan of pushing north into North Carolina to unleash a winter campaign to catch the patriots by surprise.

Cornwallis spied an opportunity to place himself between the widely-separated forces of Morgan and Greene and then crush an isolated Morgan, who possessed fewer numbers of troops and lingered more than a hundred miles from Greene's Army. Cornwallis, therefore, unleashed his most aggressive top lieutenant, Tarleton, and his elite British Legion which was augmented by other veteran units. Tarleton's vigorous pursuit toward Kings Mountain and Morgan's isolated task force set the stage for the dramatic showdown between Tarleton and General Greene's top lieutenant in the Piedmont of South Carolina, just below the North Carolina line and just west of Kings Mountain.

By mid-February, Morgan ascertained the approaching danger, and withdrew at a rapid pace. But after learning that Lieutenant Colonel Tarleton and his crack force were in fast pursuit and that he would not be able to slip away across the rain-swollen Broad River before darkness fell in this rolling land of thick forests, the savvy Morgan made a bold decision. Despite recently promoted to brigadier general and eager for action despite suffering from the ill-affects of his hard service during the arduous march to Quebec and imprisonment in Canada, Morgan planned to make a stand

and fight the much-feared Tarleton. Most of all and as revealed by the sad fate of a good many American troops, including guerrillas, in the South, Morgan could not risk being struck by Tarleton, while withdrawing and unprepared to face the blow: a recipe for certain disaster.

Now commanding light troops and more than half of General Greene's Army which contained a large percentage of Irish and Scotch-Irish, Morgan decided to make a stand at a vital crossroads with his small army of militia and battle-hardened Continental troops. The Irishman now planned to fight at an obscure grassy clearing on the west side of the dark waters of the rain-swollen Broad River. As advised by some of his officers who intimately knew the area and the suitability of making a defensive stand at "Hannah's Cowpens," this location was an ideal place to fight, consisting of relatively high and gently rolling ground and relative narrow opening in the woodlands to protect his flanks. In fact, many veterans of Kings Mountain in the ranks were familiar with the Cowpens when used as a militia assembly area. Some of these militiamen had rested at this cleared open ground on their way to vanquishing Ferguson Loyalist command.

However, defending this relatively low ground was a risky decision also because of the ever-unpredictable militiamen in the ranks, even though Morgan knew he could count on his roughly 600 Continentals. After all, Ferguson had lost his life by deciding to make a defensive stand, while commanding a disciplined command on good high ground at nearby Kings Mountain. And since the Cowpens was well-known, North Carolina, Georgia, and South Carolina militia–such as the band of patriots under Scotch-Irish General Andrew Pickens--could rally to Morgan's force at this point.

The setting that General Morgan selected to make his defensive stand was situated amid the pine woodlands known locally to the people of the northern South Carolina uplands, or the Piedmont, as the Cowpens. This carefully-chosen area was a natural meadow long utilized to pen and pasture cattle during winter on the western frontier, before the colonists drove them north up the Great Valley of Virginia to eastern markets, principally Philadelphia. This unique place was situated in a region with relatively few clearings or open ground: a sprawling, open grassy plain that stretched north for five miles to the Broad River. Morgan planned to make a fight at the Cowpens without the advantage of a high ground defensive position like Kings Mountain.

By this time, however, the prospects for American success looked less than promising because Morgan would have to face Lieutenant Colonel Tarleton and his much feared British Legion, consisting of American Loyalists. These were the finest light troops in America: hardhitting, bold, and aggressive. And no mercy could be expected from Tarleton's hard-bitten warriors, who knew how to wage a total war against their fellow Americans, soldier or civilian, in revolt. To defeat a superior opponent in terms of discipline, training and weaponry, General Morgan would have to rely upon his own skill and leadership ability to develop a masterful battle plan, especially against the ever-aggressive Tarleton, who had made a career by easily defeating Americans, especially ill-trained militia, whenever he meet them.

Envisioning an original tactical plan that was calculated to exploit Tarleton's weaknesses which were only too few, the imaginative Irishman, therefore, carefully designed a clever battle-plan. This tactical plan was carefully crafted based upon the advantages of the topography of the Cowpens, as well as sound realizations about his soldiers' fighting qualities and the tactical and psychological realities of warfare in America. Situated amid stands of dense forests, the grassy open land of the Cowpens was bordered on both ends by marshy ground, ensuring protection of Morgan's flanks. Such a fine defensive position would prevent Tarleton's cavalrymen, who were well known for outflanking, lightning strikes, and cutting patriot units to pieces on open ground like at Camden, from out-flanking Morgan's position on the open ground before the Broad River.

In order to give Lieutenant Colonel Tarlton "a decent reception," as ordered by General Greene, the forty-five-year-old "Old Wagoner" from the Emerald Isle proceeded to develop the most brilliant, imaginative, and innovative tactical plan of the American Revolution. Inspiring his men with his own unfailing common soldier approach, Morgan radiated a great deal of confidence to the young men and boys in the ranks. He repeatedly told his soldiers how easily they could defeat the much-feared Tarleton and his Legion.

To his troops, Morgan repeatedly derided the twenty-six-year-old aristocratic Briton as "Benny." But most Americans, and for good reason, knew Tarleton by his much-feared reputation as "the Butcher," "Bloody Ban," and "Bloody Tarleton." He had waged a highly successful and especially vicious brand of warfare, which was distinguished by a brutal no-quarter policy that had been first initiated by his superior, Lord Cornwallis. With typical Irish feistiness and echoing the later-day sentiments of Ireland-born Andrew Jackson before the battle of New Orleans in January 1815, Morgan swore a solemn promise to his men that lifted their confidence and spirits at the Cowpens: "On this ground I will beat Benny Tarleton or I will lay my bones." As Morgan well knew, these were exactly the kind of inspiring words that the young soldiers in the ranks, especially those with little experience, most of all wanted to hear from the revered commander.

Eager to destroy Morgan's forces with their back to the Broad River and before the Americans could escape across the river in the cold early morning hours of January 17, 1781 despite his exhausted troops having pushed rapidly in pursuit in the predawn darkness in the hope of catching Morgan by surprise, Tarleton moved his men out of the dark woodlands lining the road. Upon learning of the American's presence, he then hurriedly deployed his formations for the attack. With Morgan's first line barely 400 yards distant, he planned not to waste a minute of time, before striking a blow.

Confident of success, Tarleton prepared to unleash more than 1,000 troops upon the outnumbered militia and Continentals under the unpretentious former teamster from County Derry, Ireland. Tarleton's natural instincts were always to strike fast and hard at any opponent, especially one who was cornered: one secret of his many past successes on battlefields across the South.

Ever-the-fighter and despite the return of an illness lingering from the wintery hell of the Quebec campaign, Morgan had expected as much from his ever-aggressive adversary. This keen understanding of Tarleton's liabilities—an over-aggressive and rashness--as a military commander was part of his tactical reasoning in deciding to make a defensive stand at the Cowpens. Consequently, Morgan would exploit Tarleton's audacity to lead him into what was essentially a tactical trap. General Morgan and his men would be ready and waiting for the moment when the young Briton unleashed the aggressive tactics upon which he had won his widespread fame on one battlefield after another, the headlong attack.

Relying upon the hard-earned lessons of frontier, guerrilla, and Indian warfare and the tactics employed by him at Saratoga, General Morgan's battle-plan was not only tailored to the Cowpens' terrain and his opponent's weaknesses, but also, as important, was based upon his greatest strength, the battle-hardened Maryland, Virginia, and Delaware Continentals, while minimizing his greatest weakness, the mostly inexperienced militia.

Therefore, Morgan developed a brilliant tactical plan based upon a defense in depth. The Irishman's battle-plan called for three parallel battle-lines spread across the open ground of the Cowpens. As planned by Morgan and as ordained by the slight advantageous offered by the terrain, these defensive lines were widely-separated and out-of-sight of each other. More important, the second and third defensive lines were completely out-of-sight of Tarleton and his troops. Even more and as orchestrated by Morgan, each defensive line was progressively stronger and more advantageous to the defenders in regard to the terrain's contours than the previous line: overall, a masterful tactical plan designed by the Emerald Islander to steadily sap the strength and momentum of the inevitably British onslaught. After all, Lieutenant Colonel Tarleton was sure to unleash his troops with his typical aggressive fashion.

Morgan's carefully-thought-out tactical plan defied conventional concepts of Eighteenth Century warfare because the least reliable soldiers—in terms of standing up to hardened British regulars attacking with bayonets—were in the foremost lines, while the most reliable troops, the veteran Continentals, who were the equals to the British regulars in every way, were positioned farthest to the rear in the final line. In the first line stood North Carolina and Virginia riflemen who, armed with deadly long rifles instead of shorter-range and more inaccurate smoothbore muskets, would initially inflict some damage on Tarleton's attackers, especially in targeting enemy officers in a repeat of the performance of Morgan's rifle corps at Saratoga.

Meanwhile, South Carolina militiamen under the resourceful Colonel Andrew Pickens, a Scotch-Irish leader who commanded the largest number of militiamen at Cowpens, and Virginia militia occupied the second line. The third line consisted of the crack Continental regulars, who

130

could be depended upon the most in a crisis situation. Morgan's battle-plan ensured that each successive defensive line encountered by the attacking British would be not only stronger, but also would be composed of more reliable, veteran soldiers than the previous line.

Indeed, a thin line of carefully-picked riflemen, consisting of North Carolina militiamen under Colonel Joseph McDowell, the Scotch-Irish commander who had led the mountain men to victory over Major Ferguson and his Loyalists at Kings Mountain, and Georgia militia made-up the first line that was aligned amid the thin cover of trees. Many of these sharpshooters, especially those of Colonel McDowell, were Irish and Scotch-Irish warriors, who had fought British, Loyalists, and Native Americans for years.

A master psychologist with insights into the common man in the ranks, Morgan found novel ways to motivate his Scotch-Irish and Irish soldiers. He occasionally displayed his scarred back to show how the British treated a man--when even an ally in the French and Indian War--born in Ireland. Morgan also exploited the considerable vanity and pride of the North Carolina marksmen. Thanks to part to the victory achieved at Kings Mountain, he knew that these men loudly boasted how they were the finest sharpshooters in the army. Therefore, Morgan offered a direct challenge: by occupying the first line, they would have an opportunity to back-up their big talk about their prowess with rifles. Consequently, the Irish and Scotch-Irish from North Carolina of the first line were highly motivated to not only punish Tarleton's troops, but also to demonstrated their worth and value.

The South Carolina and Virginia militiamen, or state troops, composing the second line of defense, stood on the first rise of the gently sloping open ground of the grassy Cowpens. But without bayonets or sufficient training, Morgan knew that the militiamen of this first line would not be able to stand firm for long against the bayonets of well-trained British troops, including regular infantry, and Tarleton's hard-hitting onslaught.

Consequently, General Morgan informed his troops of his innovative battle-plan, making extra sure that everyone–from commanding officer to the most humble private–understood exactly what was expected at precisely the right moment. There could be no margin for error today at the Cowpens. The savvy Irishman, therefore, told the Georgia and North Carolina riflemen of the first line to retire to the second line, after unleashing only a few shots at the onrushing attackers. In turn, Morgan also ordered the second line of South Carolina and Virginia militiamen to fire only a few shots, before falling back around 150 yards to the third, or main, defensive line consisting of the reliable Continentals from Maryland, Delaware, and Virginia.

Here, at the last line atop a slight rise in the center of the meadow-like Cowpens, the militiamen hopefully would then rally and reload their muskets, while the Continentals held firm in the last line, and then hurriedly return to the firing line to add extra firepower at the critical moment to break the back of the enemy onslaught. With confidence and foresight, Morgan explained to the militiamen a simple tactical reality and offered a heady inducement, as he saw it, based upon the most important requirement at the Cowpens on this day of destiny: "Give them three fires, and you will be free."

All in all, General Morgan had laid a clever "tactical trap" for Tarleton at the Cowpens. The obvious weakness of the foremost American lines would only further ignite the well-known aggressiveness of Tarleton, who, sensing what seemed to be a golden tactical opportunity with the Broad River to the American's back, would charge straight into multiple and ever-stronger defensive lines. Tarleton's well-known aggressiveness would be only fueled to new heights when the first line of militiamen fell back, retiring across the open ground. Quite simply, as the British advanced ever-farther forward, this well-conceived plan guaranteed that the strength of General Morgan's defenders would steadily grow more formidable, while Tarleton's strength and momentum would steadily diminish as the advance covered more ground. Because of the lay of the land and as calculated by Morgan, Tarleton would be surprised during his advance by the sudden appearance of the second and third American defensive lines of this masterful defensive trap, as the British advanced deeper into the carefully concealed tactical lair of Morgan's defense in-depth.

Meanwhile, eager to orchestrate the seemingly all-but-assured rout of yet another seemingly ill-fated American force as at Camden and instinctively sensing the kill despite an all-night march and with his men needing rest, Tarleton issued a brutal order in this enthusiasm to reap yet another bloody victory. Confident that he could easily shatter General Morgan's line and scatter these ragtag amateur soldiers across the open ground of the Cowpens with a dawn attack as he had originally planned, Lieutenant Colonel Tarleton deemed that no quarter would be granted to the Americans, regardless of age or rank.

To increase the morale and spirits among the American troops and in part to counter an opposing commander well-known for his no-quarter policy, meanwhile, Morgan ordered his men to give the British "the Indian halloo" from the western frontier A roar of defiance erupted from the ranks of the deployed Americans, revealing their fighting spirit. Tarleton could resist no longer. As Morgan had anticipated, the British formations surged ahead with typical overconfidence born of a series of past easy victories and with colorful battle-flags fluttering in the soft mid-October sunshine.

As ordered, the large number of Irish and Scotch-Irish under the reliable Colonel Campbell in the first line, carefully picked-out targets when Tarleton's advancing troops were within 100 yards and fired. Then, they quickly loaded and fired again. More attackers fell to the ground, but they continued to surge forward with confidence and fixed bayonets. As Morgan anticipated, Campbell's Celts upheld their lofty reputation, cutting down a good many of Tarleton's officers and sergeants as directed.

However, the confidence of Tarleton's soldiers only soared higher when the first line of around 150 North Carolina and Georgia riflemen positioned in the trees suddenly gave way, and retired north across the open, grassy ground and headed toward the second militia line as ordered by Morgan, after unleashing their required two volleys. Most important, and as directed by Morgan, the withdrawing soldiers retired with discipline, firing at will to continue punishing Tarleton's elated soldiers as they advanced across the open ground.

Now, according to Morgan, the British now "came Running at us as if they Intended to eat us up." But this time there was no rout of another American force in the making as so often in the past and as the British expected with certainty. All the while, General Pickens, the ever-resourceful Scotch-Irish chieftain who commanded the second line along a slight crest some 150 yards north of the abandoned first line, had his boys ready to greet the onslaught.

At this time, the second line of North Carolina and South Carolina militiamen–the majority of Morgan's force with around 300 men--opened up and blazed away, blasting into the surging British ranks at close range as Morgan had ordered: "don't touch a trigger until you see the whites of their eyes." As with his troops of the first line, Morgan also implored them to cut down both officers and sergeants, and they obeyed with deadly efficiency.

After firing their required two or three shots that caused additional destruction in the steadily advancing British formations, Pickens' militiamen then retired back to the main line of Continentals and around their left flank to quickly reassemble in the rear. Along with the ever-reliable Continental troops, Colonel William Washington's band of cavalrymen were held in reserve behind the third defensive line around 150 yards north, or uphill, from the vacated second line, and out-of-sight of the approaching British. Sensing a decisive victory had already been won, Tarleton's troops, now cheering in triumph, rushed forward with new enthusiasm, but without order or discipline as Morgan had hoped. Tarleton and his men believed that the militia's withdraw indicated the complete rout of the Americans–seemingly another Camden fiasco in the making--and that a decisive victory was now inevitable.

As General Morgan, the old rifleman and French and Indian War veteran, had envisioned, the seasoned Maryland, Virginia, and Delaware Continentals held firm in the face of Tarleton's onslaught. Now they exchanged a hot fire with the British, unleashing disciplined, close-range volleys that wrecked havoc. As expected, the volleys erupting from the Continental line were effective in knocking down a good many of Tarleton's young men and boys, blunting the attack's momentum.

In the noisy confusion of battle and amid the drifting layers of smoke, however, an accidental withdrawal a short distance by the Continental troops, when the company on the right flank of the battle-line attempted to shift positions by refusing the flank to parry a threat, now only caused the British to surge forward with more wild abandon. During the tumult, some patriot captains of companies mistakenly believed that the sudden movement on the right flank was a withdrawal and likewise moved back. However, the confusion in the American ranks, ironically, actually worked to Morgan's advantage amid the confusing smoke of battle and noise. An apparent British success in what was already a reckless attack now made the British only more vulnerable

135

in what had become a wild charge lacking order or discipline.

Meanwhile, to restore order, General Morgan rallied and reformed the militiamen to the cry of, "Form, form, my brave fellows [and] Give them one more fire and the day is ours." As in leading his charging soldiers forward through Quebec's streets in a driving snowstorm in late December 1775, General Morgan continued to inspire his men to greater exertions. Morgan's leadership skill worked magic at the Cowpens, as at Quebec. At the last moment, the rallied riflemen and militiamen reinforced the Continentals, ensuring that even additional concentrated firepower was delivered upon the attacking British, who, with losses increasing with each passing minute, were now at their weakest and most vulnerable.

Then, to maximize the shock, Colonel Washington's cavalrymen successfully counterattacked to stabilize Morgan's left by striking Tarleton's cavalry head-on. All the while, Morgan continued to steady the defense of the final line, ordering a volley fired into the faces of the onrushing British. Then, Lieutenant Colonel John Eager Howard, from the port of Baltimore, Maryland on the Patapsco River, ordered his Maryland Continentals to charge with the bayonet, while the rallied militia struck Tarleton's left. The charging Tarleton's Legion was now the victim of a double envelopment. While the hard-hit Legionaries fled the field in defeat, the British cannoneers remained defiantly beside their guns. Having never known defeat, these young artillerymen refused to surrender their beloved field pieces. Therefore, these determined gunners had to be shot down and bayoneted almost to a man.

Most important, the counterattacking Maryland Continentals caught the redcoats by surprise and shattered all British hopes for an easy victory as so often achieved in the past. In a reversal of roles, Washington's cavalry now chased Tarleton's men, including the famed "Green Horse," in a wild pursuit down the narrow, dirt road and through the pine forests and fallow fields tinged in winter's drab hue of brown.

As carefully orchestrated by General Morgan, one of the most impressive American victories of the American Revolution was won in dramatic fashion at an obscure place in the South Carolina Piedmont called Cowpens. A full three-fourths of Tarleton's force was either killed, wounded, or captured in the British rout at the Cowpens.

Among the common soldiers, one Irishman who distinguished himself on this day was Thomas Brandon, whose family had migrated from Ireland to the western frontier of Pennsylvania. The Brandon family had been part of "a colony of Irish Presbyterians," who then migrated to South Carolina from Pennsylvania. At Cowpens, Brandon, who was a veteran of Kings Mountain, personally killed three of Tarleton's hated dragoons with his saber in bitter hand-to-hand fighting.

During the darkest days of the war in the South, the unexpected American victory by the small patriot force commanded by an uneducated, unorthodox Ireland-born general from the western frontier restored badly-shattered confidence to patriots across the war-torn South. For the first time, the seemingly invincible Lieutenant Colonel Tarleton had been vanquished and his prized and well-honed Legion defeated in decisive fashion in a tactical masterpiece by a gifted general from northern Ireland.

In fact, the famed Tarleton Legion, the "flower" of Lord Cornwallis's Army, had not only been beaten by the innovative tactics and leadership ability of the "Old Wagoner," but also suffered "a whale of a licking." This was an appropriate analogy employed by Morgan, who had repaid the British in full at Cowpens for the 500 lashes–he estimated only 499--that he had received from the British lash. New hope and optimism for a successful revolution was revived across the Southern colonies, after one of the most one-sided victories of the American Revolution. Increasing numbers of patriots across America began to believe that decisive victory was only a matter of time. Consequently, the battle of Cowpens was a major turning point of the American Revolution. The army of General Cornwallis, the main British force in the South, had lost its most vital and energetic component, all of its crack light infantry and its most effective cavalry under its most aggressive top lieutenant with the decimation of Tarleton's Legion at Cowpens. Quite simply, Cornwallis lost his invaluable eyes and ears at Cowpens.

Thanks to his tactical masterpiece, Morgan had almost singlehandedly thwarted British strategic ambitions and Lord Cornwallis' grandiose dream of the conquest of North Carolina. The unexpected–almost unbelievable-victory at Cowpens helped to pave the way for additional future British setbacks in the South, while setting the stage nine months later for the final drama to be played out at with Lord Cornwallis's surrender at Yorktown, Virginia, in October 1781.

A lowly Irishman from County Derry, Ireland, and the remote Virginia backwoods who was ever-mindful of the bitter legacies of Irish history and eager to avenge that tragic Irish past which had tormented the hearts and souls of the Irish people for generations, General Morgan had played more distinguished leadership roles and for a longer period, from Quebec to Cowpens, 1775 to 1783, than perhaps any other officer of the Continental Army. But no contribution was more important in the winning of America's independence than the brilliant victory orchestrated by a former Irish teamster, who created a tactical masterpiece an obscure meadow known as the Cowpens so long ago.

ABOUT THE AUTHO

DR. PHILLIP THOMAS TUCKER earned a Ph.D. in American History from St. Louis University, St. Louis, Missouri, in 1990. Since that time, he has been employed as a historian for the United States Air Force. In total, he has written or edited more than twenty books on various aspects of the American experience, focusing primarily on African American, Irish, women's, Southern, and Civil War history. He won two awards, one national and one state, for the best book in Southern history in 1993. Tucker currently works as a United States Air Force historian in Washington, D.C.

Bibliographic Note

Unfortunately, there are no lengthy studies or definitive accounts of the vital role played by the Irish and the Scotch-Irish in the American Revolution and their key contributions in helping to win the independence of a new nation.

However, only too brief glimpses of the important achievements of the Irish can be found here and there in little more than footnotes and in brief, scattered references from hundreds of secondary works, both old and recent, about the American Revolution. Combined with primary source material from archives and a good many contemporary newspaper accounts, principally from the *Maryland Gazette*, Annapolis, Maryland, these obscure references from a good many and wide variety of secondary sources, both old and new, have been utilized to tell the dramatic story of the Irish and the Scotch-Irish during some of the most decisive battles of the revolutionary war.

Made in the USA
Middletown, DE
28 September 2021

49232088R00080